# DEAF
# PEDDLER

# DEAF PEDDLER

## Confessions
## of an Inside Man

Dennis S. Buck

Gallaudet University Press
Washington, D.C.

Gallaudet University Press
Washington, DC 20002

© 2000 by Gallaudet University.
All rights reserved. Published 2000
Printed in Canada

Library of Congress Cataloging-in-Publication Data

Buck, Dennis S.
  Deaf peddler : confessions of an inside man / Dennis S. Buck.
    p. cm.
  Includes bibliographical references.
  ISBN 1-56368-096-3
  1. Buck, Dennis S.   2. Peddlers and peddling—United States—
  Biography.   3. Deaf men—United States—Biography.   I. Title.
  HF5459.U6 B83 2000
  362.4'2'092—dc21
  [B]

                                                    00-031624

# Contents

# Foreword

These past several decades have been a time of advance for the deaf community in the United States. Deaf and hearing individuals alike have learned about the history and culture of the American deaf community through an increasing number of movies, plays, books, and more recently, websites. In addition, deaf adults, like women, African-Americans, and other minorities, have invigorated their efforts to counter prejudice and discrimination in society at large. Many in the nation closely followed deaf students who, in 1988, led the bold campaign that galvanized deaf citizens and brought Gallaudet University its first deaf president. Less prominent, but no less significant, are the ongoing campaigns to promote American Sign Language (ASL) and increase the educational opportunities of deaf children. Similarly, deaf adults joined with others on behalf of the Americans with Disabilities Act (ADA), whose passage in 1990 established workplace rights for deaf and other qualified adults. These efforts have increased the linguistic, artistic, educational, and employment opportunities for deaf individuals—and enriched the nation.

Given the efforts that have made these advances possible—as well as the obstacles remaining before deaf Americans—it should be no surprise if some deaf and hearing readers are troubled, if not angered, by this book. Paradoxically, Dennis Buck, the articulate and self-revealing author, would likely understand any bewilderment or betrayal engendered by this brief and engrossing autobiographical narrative. It is possible that several readers may have seen or even encountered the author at his preferred work site for much of the 1990s: Chicago's O'Hare International Airport. As the title indicates, Dennis Buck was neither a uniformed concessionaire nor a harried airline employee, but a self-described entrepreneur who put in long, hard days to offer his varied wares to travelers in one of the world's largest and busiest thoroughfares.

The author, however, was not a typical vendor who might sell candy, magazines, or other sundry items at inflated prices. Rather, as the author himself acknowledges, critics will likely charge that for ten years Dennis Buck sold *himself* or, more precisely, exploited his identity as a deaf, sign language-using inhabitant of a wheelchair, to sustain a steady—even lucrative—career as a peddler.[1] Moreover, it can be asserted that

---

1. See Robert Scott, *The Making of Blind Men: A Study of Adult Socialization* (New York: Russell Sage Foundation, 1969), 110–12. For example, Scott argues that blind beggars "exploit for their own eco-

the author hurt others besides himself. Critics will contend that the author's public activities may have damaged the standing of the deaf community.

∞

Peddlers have typically been confined to a marginal existence at the periphery of economic activity and cultural life in the United States. From colonial times through industrialization and up to the current age of globalization, popular culture has almost always portrayed peddlers and peddling in a negative light. At times, peddlers have been characterized as persistent and unsavory dispensers of items both spurious and necessary: "snake oil" in the nineteenth-century frontier and flimsy umbrellas in contemporary New York City. At other times, peddlers have been depicted as troubled individuals a few steps removed from begging or homelessness. Black-and-white photographs of unemployed men selling apples or pencils on street corners during the Depression, for example, have become veritable icons. Rarely, if ever, have peddlers been considered examples of favorable entrepreneurial activity. Moreover, few in government, academia, social service organizations, or society at large have sought to study either peddlers or the dynamics of exchange between peddler and the public. As a result, peddling remains a phenomenon in which fact is not easily distinguished from folklore.

---

nomic gain the emotions and fears sighted people have about blindness."

The organized deaf community, deeply troubled by these stereotypes, has consistently condemned peddling. Indeed, it may be accurate to say that among many deaf adults, the term *peddler* is as much epithet as occupation. To these critics, a deaf peddler exploits the erroneous pity of naïve, hearing passersby.

Dennis Buck's story seems to confirm some of these stereotypes as it questions others. At one level, this is a compelling story of one man's "coming of age," in which he transcends external challenges and internal frailties to emerge—in the end—a respected member of his community. Certainly, readers will be heartened by the author's description of his youth and young adulthood. A hardworking, intelligent, even accomplished, learner, Buck had talents and abilities that brought him success at a university that is the hub for deaf students from around the globe. Many will be enlightened and impressed by his determined actions and attitudes following a motorcycle accident that left him paralyzed below the chest. Throughout this period he regularly earned the respect of family, peers, and employers. At the same time, however, the author led a secret life that could have destroyed these accomplishments.

Most readers will probably find Dennis Buck's years as a peddler to be the most noteworthy section of the book. On the one hand, this candid narrative is an engrossing journey that provides readers an "insider's" perspective of this much-maligned activity. On the other hand, in his deepening self-disappointment and eventual rejection of peddling, Buck seems to confirm

the claim that peddling corrodes the peddler's character as it insults, if not injures, the larger group or community to which the peddler belongs. Whatever the
ethical shortcomings of peddling, some readers may
conclude that the author is, in fact, independent and industrious. Although Buck's experiences and commen-
tary raise more questions than his book answers, this
work is sure to provoke much needed discussion, de-
bate and, perhaps, further study among and between
deaf and hearing readers.

What is known about the origins and activities of deaf
peddlers? A sketch of the employment history of the
deaf community provides a starting point to this query.
Consistent with other minority groups in the United
States, deep divisions in employment have regularly
separated deaf adults. State, federal, and school-based
surveys and data from the mid-nineteenth century
through the 1950s, for example, indicate that racial,
class, educational, and gender fault lines have divided
the deaf community. Not surprisingly, deaf women and
men of color, especially those from southern or other
states with historically small educational budgets, have
been relegated to marginal positions in agriculture, industry, and service industries. In recent decades, deaf
women, like hearing women, have enjoyed slightly
greater educational and employment opportunities.
Among white males, access to advanced technical
training or college has often led to the widest range of
vocational opportunities. Recent college and univer-

sity-based programs, backed by governmental measures intended to limit discrimination, have contributed to the growth of a deaf middle class that enjoys unequaled vocational opportunities.

In addition to these gains, there remains cause for concern. Many educational and vocational programs across the nation remain poorly funded, while some states are seeking to cap if not reduce funding for "special education." At the same time, despite the passage of the ADA, evidence seems to indicate that the most vulnerable deaf workers—those with rudimentary educational training—face discrimination and few job opportunities. For these men and women, underemployment and unemployment remains a fact of life. Logic suggests that many peddlers have come from this class of poorly educated adults.

The records of state, regional, and national associations and the deaf newspapers from the nineteenth and twentieth centuries indicate that broad economic disruptions contributed to peddling.[2] Apparently, some peddlers never attended school while others peddled after their agricultural or artisan-based livelihoods were threatened by industrialization. Still others peddled during the nation's intermittent depressions or after mass layoffs. In the late 1890s, for example, one deaf

---

2. For an overview, see Jack Gannon, *Deaf Heritage: A Narrative History of Deaf America* (Silver Spring, Md.: National Association of the Deaf, 1981): 255–59. Gannon's brief discussion is insightful and relevant today.

writer argued that unemployment and poverty among deaf workers was worsened by the "deadly prejudice" of industrial leaders who refused to hire deaf applicants.[3] Another newspaper article reinforced these perceptions, as it noted the death of Joseph Quinn, a successful cabinetmaker, compelled to the streets after the business in which he labored shut down. Unable to find gainful employment, he peddled soap on the streets of Baltimore, fell ill, and died a pauper.[4] In the midst of the nation's worst depression, another deaf job seeker echoed these themes in 1933. Unemployed for four years, Frank Thompson, a printer with two decades of experience, wrote the administration of President Franklin Delano Roosevelt to ask for assistance in finding work and to censure private employers who refused to hire deaf workers. Forced to "rove the streets forth and back" in a vain effort to find work, Thompson closed his letter by conceding he had turned to peddling.[5]

---

3. Hypatia Boyd, "Plea For the Deaf," *Deaf Mute's Journal*, March 27, 1899, p. 4. Boyd cites the correspondence of one unemployed man: "What is the use of an education if when you leave school you cannot get a situation? Do you know what it is to be in want of food? To have your wife and babies driven out, penniless and thinly clad, into a howling snowstorm by an irate landlord?"

4. "Baltimore," *Deaf Mute's Journal*, March 24, 1998, p.4.

5. Letter from Frank Thompson to General Hugh Johnson, September 16, 1933 (Washington, D.C., National Archives, Record Group 69: National Recovery Administration, Folder 567: Handicapped—Deaf). Twelve days later, Thompson received a reply that indicated the administration had moved to provide jobs for "per-

In addition to adults who reluctantly turned to the streets, historical sources reveal that other deaf adults actively pursued peddling as a chosen vocation. The actions of an itinerant peddler named Henry Bartho-momay seem representative. Barthomomay apparently frequented a circuit of Midwestern cities, peddling self-described "educational" cards that featured the manual alphabet. In addition to illustrating fingerspelling, they also explained "[t]hese cards have been printed for the purpose of assisting me, a Deaf Mute, in making a living. Will you kindly buy one? Pay ANY price you wish. THANK YOU!"[6] For much of the twentieth century, the corps of professional peddlers also included hearing adults who posed as deaf peddlers.[7] Although there is

---

sons who are limited in their earning power through physical defects, age or other infirmities." Unfortunately, the New Deal programs never established a coherent or uniform approach to deaf or other adults with disabilities. For example, the Civilian Conservation Corps refused to consider deaf workers, and the Work Progress Administration was uneven in its hiring actions. See Robert M. Buchanan, *Illusions of Equality: Deaf Americans in School and Factory, 1850–1950* (Washington, D.C.: Gallaudet University Press, 1999), 85–101.

6. "Wanted." *The Frat*, November 1947, p. 8.

7. For an overview on impostors, see Lowell Myers, *The Law and the Deaf* (Washington, D.C.: United States Department of Health Education and Welfare, 1967), 144–48. For a specific example of the views and actions of a state organization, see "The Minnesota Law against Impostors," *The Companion*, December 13, 1916, p. 7. For an example of a deaf leader confronting alleged impostors, see "An Unusual Experience," *The Companion*, March 8, 1934, p. 2.

no way of knowing exactly how many individuals assumed these roles, the phenomenon was sufficiently pervasive, especially during the first half of the century, for deaf leaders in the National Association of the Deaf (NAD) and several states to pursue legislation intended to prohibit impersonation.[8]

State as well as national leaders at the NAD and the National Fraternal Society of the Deaf (NFSD) led vigorous public campaigns against "professional" peddlers during the twentieth century. In 1913, for example, some leaders in the NAD favored making it a crime for deaf adults to "ask for assistance on account of deafness."[9] More often, deaf leaders publicly condemned peddlers. Deaf leaders in metropolitan New York City effectively joined humor and scorn in their effort to distance themselves from an upsurge of peddling that followed widespread industrial layoffs at the close of World War II. A mock job advertisement entitled "Peddlers Wanted" sought to warn and shame would-be peddlers: "Good job, cleaning jails, polishing rails, free lodging on a hard bed, good meals on a watery diet 500

---

8. The NAD established a committee to consider the issue of impostors in 1911. By the 1940s, NAD officials generally agreed that this trend had diminished. See the NAD's convention proceedings from these decades.

9. "Mr. Howard's Report on Impostors," *Proceedings of the Tenth Convention of the National Association of the Deaf* (Olathe, Kans.: Independent Publishing Company, 1913), 104–106, 146.

calories per day. Send in reference on education and experience to [the Empire State Association of the Deaf.]"[10]

Within the organizations of the national deaf community, it was not uncommon for deaf educators and leaders to publicly ostracize peddlers and some unemployed adults.[11] Ever mindful of their responsibilities as exemplars to deaf youth and hearing adults (including potential employers), deaf leaders vigorously condemned peddling. The comments of James Smith, president of the Minnesota Association of the Deaf and a teacher at the state residential school in 1885, are severe yet representative. In a speech before fellow members of the state association he advised, "[i]f a deaf stranger from another place comes among you, meet him as a brother, offer to help him get work." But "if he does not work, if he prefers to depend upon charity —then regard him as your enemy, and treat him as such."[12]

As these illustrations indicate, many deaf adults understood that their opportunities as workers were

---

10. "Peddlers Wanted," *Empire State News*, June 1946, p. 1.

11. For examples, see "Deaf and Dumb Laborers," *New York Times*, August 27, 1881, p. 5; Editorial, *Deaf Mute's Journal*, October 19, 1882, p. 2.

12. James L. Smith, "The Progress of the Deaf," *Proceedings of the Second Convention of the Minnesota Association of the Deaf* (Faribault, Minn.: Minnesota State School for the Deaf, Printing Office, 1890), 26–28. Regarding Smith, see "James Lewis Smith," *Companion*, April 20, 1933, 1–26.

linked, in part, to the perceptions of hearing society. As most hearing adults likely had little interaction with deaf adults, deaf leaders feared that the example of one peddler could threaten the status of industrious adults.[13] In 1897, one leader explained that the public "cannot be expected to know of the great army of deaf-mute workers, whose industry, integrity and capacity make them unobtrusive and model citizens." Sixty years later, another writer worried that the "accomplishments of the nation's deaf citizens 'mean very little,' to a person who has been approached by a peddler."[14]

Questioning the effectiveness of censure, leaders and writers have also worked to undercut peddling by directly assisting adults hurt by broad economic dislocations.[15] At the 1883 NAD convention, for example,

---

13. Although deaf leaders have regularly communicated this fear, there remains little research-based evidence that peddling has ever negatively influenced the attitudes or actions of hearing employers. Instead, the majority of surveys indicate that discriminatory employers have typically claimed that communicating with deaf employees would be burdensome. In fact, employers have more regularly concluded that deaf employees have proven themselves to be more industrious and efficient than their hearing cohorts. See, Buchanan, *Illusions of Equality* and *Deaf Students and Workers in the United States, 1800–1950* (Ph.D. diss., University of Wisconsin, 1995).

14. "Editorial," *Deaf Mute's Journal*, July 29, 1897, p. 2; Lowell J. Myers, "The Legal Column," *Silent Worker*, September 1960, 36–37.

15. Jersey Blue (pseud.) to *Deaf Mute's Journal*, September 29, 1881, p. 4.

Thomas Brown, founder of the New England Gallaudet Association, argued that inadequate vocational training threatened the status of all deaf workers. Without upgraded training, Brown charged, more men would peddle or beg in order to survive.[16] Fifty years later, in the midst of the Depression, deaf leaders publicly acknowledged that difficult economic conditions led industrious adults to peddle. At the 1934 NAD convention, Akron, Ohio's Kreigh Ayers noted that a "good many" of "honest and able" adults had been forced to "peddle, beg or panhandle to exist."[17] More recently, deaf leaders have regularly urged peddlers to seek assistance from state rehabilitation services and other sources.[18]

16. *Proceedings of the Second National Convention of Deaf-Mutes* (New York: New York Institution for the Deaf and Dumb, 1884), 16–19. While one member sided with Brown, requesting that organizations assist unemployed workers, a second participant demanded swift punishment of tramps and peddlers. Apparently, even the respected Brown could not sway his unyielding peers to consider including these unfortunate adults in their community. For background, see "Biographical Sketch of Thomas Brown," *Deaf Mute's Journal*, January 21, 1880, p. 2.

17. Kreigh Ayers, in "Impostor Bureau," *Proceedings of the Seventeenth Triennial Convention of the National Association of the Deaf* (n.p., 1913), p. 40.

18. Lowell J. Myers, "The Legal Column," *Silent Worker*, November 1960, 12–13; Roger Falberg, "Peddling Revisited," *The Deaf American*, December 1967, 11–12.

While Dennis Buck's tale demonstrates that peddling may never be completely eradicated, evidence seems to indicate that it has been greatly reduced.[19] Prodded by deaf and other adults with disabilities, American popular culture has increasingly provided complex and rich representations of deaf adults that can lessen the unfounded paternalism upon which peddling depends. Within the deaf community, the unheralded efforts of deaf leaders at the local, state, regional, and national level continue to improve educational, vocational, and employment opportunities for deaf adults. Ultimately, these varied advances—including the author's eventual redemption—are rooted in a powerful shared identity and collective ethos at the core of the deaf community. While we can make allowance for his gender bias, the words of Edward Hodgson remain relevant. As he explained in 1905, at the turn of the century, "No deaf man lives for himself alone."[20]

ROBERT M. BUCHANAN
Professor of History
Goddard College
Plainfield, Vermont

19. Telephone interview with NFSD director Al Van Nevel, February 16, 2000.
20. "Editorial," *Deaf Mute's Journal*, November 9, 1905, p. 2.

# Acknowledgments

First of all, I would like to thank the entire group of peddlers whose stories are featured in this book. Without them and without Don, I would not have this story to tell. If I hadn't come to know the peddling life firsthand, perhaps I wouldn't have been as motivated to better myself through education, and I wouldn't have gotten my master's degree and a decent job.

A special thanks goes to Kim Gibson-Harman, my talented ghostwriter, who helped make this book happen. Without her assistance and knowledge of deafness and the Deaf community, this book would never have been published.

Thanks to my parents, Melvin and Marion Buck, who were very supportive and encouraged me to stop peddling. They supported my career goals as I went to graduate school and finished this book.

Thanks to Gallaudet University Archives, which maintains a significant collection of newspaper clippings and other articles related to deaf peddlers, as well as Bud Long's pamphlets about peddling. These materials helped expand my understanding of the history of deaf peddling.

Many, many thanks to Gallaudet University Press for believing that others might be interested in my story, and to Tima Smith for polishing my manuscript and preparing it for publication.

And most importantly, thanks to my wonderful wife, Rosanne, who always gives me so much support and who has stood by me throughout the development of this book. Her two boys, Andrew and Philip, were there during the final stages of my work—thanks to them also. Without their continuous support, encouragement, and sacrifices, none of this would have been possible.

# Prologue

*It's 5:40 on a Friday evening. Imagine yourself sitting in a crowded gate area at O'Hare International Airport in Chicago. It's been a tough four days at a trade show, and a tough three nights attending meetings and entertaining clients. You're tired, eager to see your family. But at least the trade show was a success. As you wait for your flight home to be called, a man approaches you. He doesn't say anything, just holds out a small brochure that says something about deaf education.*

*Oh great, you think impatiently. This is just what you don't need right now. But then you realize this man must be deaf, poor guy. He looks clean cut, "normal," and not at all like a vagrant. In all your years in the corporate world, you've only known one deaf worker, Jimmy, who worked in the mailroom. You look at the pamphlet. It has pictures of signs and fingerspelling, and is stapled to a tiny tool set in a plastic case.*

*There's an awkward moment. Does he want you to keep this? The silence between you is touched by both pity and irritation. You look back at the pamphlet and read, $2 donation. You want to end this encounter, but you want to do it kindly*

*so you fish two dollars out of your wallet and hand it to him.*
*He accepts the money with a smile, mouths "thank you" and*
*moves on. Though the encounter took no more than a minute*
*and a half, it's made you think. You find that it feels good to*
*have helped out a poor deaf guy who can't work.*

∞

From 1985 to 1996 I participated in thousands of such
encounters, despite the fact that deaf peddling had
never even been part of my vocabulary—not as a child
growing up on a farm in Ohio, not as a straight-A student in high school, and not as a college undergraduate.
Once I did discover peddling, it was only a weekend
job—but one which usually tripled my income.

I peddled mainly in airports, malls, and restaurants.
The people I approached with my wares knew two
things about me: that I was deaf and that I got around
in a wheelchair. What they didn't know was that they
were dealing with a hardworking, former farm boy
with a bachelor's degree and a pilot's license. They
didn't know that I was a computer engineer during the
week, or that I was preparing for graduate work. Most
people treated me with a mixture of impatience and
pity, but there were a few who showed genuine concern
and others who reacted with outright hostility.

For example, one Sunday morning in Chicago I was
peddling at O'Hare International Airport. I approached
a gate area with only a few people scattered about. A
peddler likes crowds, a situation in which he or she can
make the most money in the shortest period of time. But
for some reason, I decided to give it a try. I passed out

my wares, one to a man of about forty who struck me as interesting. There was something subtly watchful about him, and when I made my rounds again to see if I had any takers, he pulled out a gold money clip engraved with an initial and dramatically pulled a one-hundred dollar bill off the stack. I thought he was going to be a smart aleck and ask if I had change for the hundred, something that did happen on occasion. Instead, he folded the bill and handed it to me discreetly. I raised my eyebrows and mouthed the words, *thank you*, signing it at the same time. He grinned and nodded.

At the opposite side of the spectrum was the body builder I approached at a mall. He was eating dinner with a young woman, and I left my pamphlet on his table and went off as I usually do. I saw him look at the pamphlet, pick it up, and tear it into little pieces. He was a big guy, well over six feet, and he must have weighed three hundred pounds. Still, I went over and asked if he wanted to buy the pamphlet, which was now shredded. His attitude was less than cordial. It had been a long day, and I made a sign that clearly indicated the size of his brain for destroying my wares. He stood up, furious—ready, I thought, to attack me, a regular-sized guy in a wheelchair. But instead he lightly hit my head and ran off.

If all the people I approached had known that I often earned $200 to $300 a day peddling, in addition to my regular job or government benefits—if they'd known these things, would they still have bought my wares? Probably not. But that is the paradox of being a deaf peddler, an admittedly cynical manipulation of the hearing community's misunderstanding and ignorance of deafness and deaf people.

The dichotomy between the person I knew I was and the person that hearing people assumed I was filled me with a growing sense of dissonance. Ultimately, it compelled me to tell my story—not only for myself, but for the bright peddlers, who are severely underestimated; for the less fortunate peddlers, who could live in a more dignified way; and for the hearing people who naïvely peel off the dollar bills . . . so they will understand and stop.

# CHAPTER ONE
# History of Deaf Peddling

The word "peddler" is derived from the Middle English *ped*, or basket. A peddler was one who carried his wares in a ped. To most people, the word conjures up an image of someone travelling from village to village with a cart laden with household items and tools, and one might think that being a deaf peddler is the same thing. But deaf peddlers sell their wares quite differently from hearing peddlers.

Unlike a hearing salesman who approaches a customer at home and may spend a lot of time extolling his products' benefits, I approached customers in a public place. I handed them a small flyer or a trinket, walked away, and returned a few minutes later to either reclaim the item or collect cash for it.

Both peddlers and traveling salesmen have been around for a long time. In the nineteenth century, neither was an unusual profession. Both hearing and deaf individuals traveled by foot, on horseback, and by train to sell their wares. In each town, they went door to door selling small items, such as first aid and sewing kits.

In sparsely populated areas, these salespeople provided goods that otherwise would have been difficult to come by.[1]

Because prevailing attitudes over the past two centuries have identified deaf people as mentally inferior, employability has been a major problem. Selling or peddling was a viable career option because it allowed one to be self-employed. Prior to the 1970s, without the safety net of Supplemental Security Income (SSI) and Social Security Disability Insurance (SSDI), deaf employees—thankful for any work at all—remained in insulting, oppressive jobs for years without complaint.[2] To ensure they would not have to interact with the public, deaf people were often given jobs in the back room as dishwashers, shoemakers, or assembly-line workers. They frequently worked for less money than their hearing counterparts. In the vernacular of deaf culture, they

1. See, for example, Timothy B. Spears, *100 Years on the Road: The Traveling Salesman in American Culture* (New Haven, Conn.: Yale University Press, 1995).

2. Paul C. Higgins, *Outsiders in a Hearing World: A Sociology of Deafness* (Beverly Hills, Calif.: Sage Publications, 1980), 104–5. Most people think of Social Security as a form of income for retired people aged sixty-five or older who have worked for many years and paid into the system. But Social Security programs also provide income for people with disabilities. Since deafness is considered a disability under this program, deaf people are eligible for benefits. The two Social Security programs most widely used by the deaf are Supplemental Security Income (SSI) and Social Security Disability Insurance (SSDI).

were said to be leading a "no good" life, a term which described the unemployed as well as those stuck in low level jobs with no future.

A deaf person leading a "no good" life was ripe for recruitment by peddler organizers. A peddler organizer is called a "cow" because of the way the organizational structure is signed: one person at the top and several branches coming down, like the udder of a cow. People mired in the circumstances of their lives—such as deaf people unable to find work or working in dead-end jobs—were exactly who the cow was looking for. The cow would offer to train them and transport them to places where they could peddle. The big money, of course, was not all kept by the peddlers; the cow often kept as much as 90 percent of their earnings.

Gullible types who quietly accepted this sort of arrangement were easily recruited. Once trapped in the peddling lifestyle, it was nearly impossible to go back to a job in the hearing world, to less money and no chance of advancement. The cow provided people with housing, food, and a sense of security not readily available to deaf people in those days. Could they get a better deal elsewhere? What other options did they have? Totally dependent on the cow, with no driver's license, no car, no savings, peddling became the only game in town.

In *Deaf Heritage: A Narrative History of Deaf America*, Jack Gannon cited a letter published in an 1874 issue of *Deaf-Mute Advance* which decried the existence of deaf peddlers. The letter urged deaf adults to repay their debt to the society that educated them by becoming productive, tax-paying citizens.[3] Some states during the nineteenth century had laws against tramps and beggars, although exceptions were made for "the deaf and other unfortunate classes of humanity."[4]

There was an upsurge in peddling after the Second World War. Wartime employment shortages meant that almost any deaf person who wanted a job could find one, but most deaf workers were laid off when war-related manufacturing came to a halt and returning soldiers reclaimed their jobs. There was no vocational rehabilitation system at this time, and so recently unemployed deaf workers had a tough time finding new jobs. Gannon further credits the increase in deaf peddling to a postwar feeling of prosperity and generosity, which made peddling very lucrative.

According to Bud Long, a deaf peddler and author writing in the late 1970s, peddling became a viable alternative to taking a poorly paying job. He viewed peddling as a way to keep deaf people off welfare, and considered peddlers to be entrepreneurs. He defined deaf peddlers as "deaf persons who sell products directly to the public in order to earn a living." Although he noted that deaf peddlers could pay Social Security taxes or pay into a retirement account, he believed many had no

3. Jack R. Gannon, *Deaf Heritage: A Narrative History of Deaf America* (Silver Spring, Md.: National Association of the Deaf, 1981).
4. Ibid., 103.

intention of retiring because of their love for their work, with all its walking and fresh air.[5]

The postwar peddling boom was short lived, however. Complaints began to surface about peddlers with an "attitude problem." The public didn't seem to mind the peddling so much as the way some peddlers reacted to being refused. There were complaints about peddlers slamming doors and using threatening facial expressions—behaviors which undoubtedly reinforced the stereotype of deaf people as a primitive lot who should be feared as well as pitied.[6]

Yet in the 1950s, a deaf peddler could earn anywhere from $20 to a $100 a day, a very attractive wage. The earnings were decent enough to entice hearing people into the deaf peddling trade.[7] A news story from Pasadena, California, for example, tells of a peddler who assaulted someone who made a snide comment behind his back.[8]

In response to growing public hostility towards deaf peddlers, the NAD began an anti-peddling campaign. The NAD also feared the sudden upsurge in

---

5. Long, *Everything about Deaf Peddlers*, 11.

6. See, for example, B. Gold, "The District Line," *The Washington Post*, 7 June 1973, 6(F); S. Hatfield, "Rude Salesman," *Cleveland Ohio Press*, 3 March 1955; T. Kelly, "Our Town: Lesson for the Day," *The Washington Daily News*, 17 September 1962.

7. ABC cards typically illustrated the fingerspelled alphabet of American Sign Language.

8. "4,000 Fake Deaf Mutes Prey on the Public; One of Them Tells the Story," *Milwaukee Wisconsin Journal*, 21 March 1956.

peddling would cause a backslide toward the old stereotypes. The last thing the association wanted was for employers to view deaf people as uneducable and unable to hold a regular job. The NAD, the National Fraternal Society of the Deaf, deaf schools, and state organizations all wrote letters to regional chambers of commerce making clear their distaste for deaf peddling.[9]

The NAD also issued statements declaring its opposition to deaf peddling.[10] One such press release was titled, "The Deaf Do Not Need to Peddle or Beg." The statement explained, "The deaf of the nation are engaged in a widespread fight to eliminate organized begging and peddling among the unprincipled element and in this struggle they need the help of educators and all friends of the deaf."[11]

The NAD encouraged business owners to throw peddlers out whenever they saw them. The association also made it clear that most of the materials sold by ped-

9. Gannon, *Deaf Heritage*.
10. See "Better Business Bureau Warns Public Against Solicitations," *The Bakersfield Californian*, 2 April 1955; "Don't give," *The New Mexico Progress*, May 1959, 16–17; J. Garretson, "Warning on Deaf Peddlers," *Cincinnati Ohio Times-Star*, 16 May 1955; J. Garretson, "Woman Located At Last," *Cincinnati Ohio Times-Star*, 1 June 1955; and National Association of the Deaf, "Stop This Racket!" [brochure], Silver Spring, Md., 1995.
11. Gannon, *Deaf Heritage*.

dlers were available for free through deaf clubs.[12] The NAD's was not the only voice speaking out at that time against deaf peddling. In 1955, J. Garretson, a *Cincinnati Times-Star* columnist, advised readers to help "by refusing to give money to these disgusting specimens of humanity."[13]

Such aggressive appeals met with success. Some states, including Wisconsin, enacted legislation specifically designed to thwart deaf peddlers.[14] Other states, such as California, included deaf peddling in legislation which prohibited solicitation by those not associated with a non-profit organization or those using a "real or feigned handicap" to solicit sales.[15] From 1955 to about 1979, many newspapers reported arrests of deaf peddlers. They were usually fined $10—a significant amount in 1955—although jail time was not uncommon. Sentences ranged from one to forty-five days, the longer sentences handed out to repeat offenders.

Despite public criticism, deaf peddlers plied their trade into the twentieth century and many continue to do so today. Yet information about deaf peddlers is

---

12. Ibid.

13. J. Garretson, 1955.

14. "All the More Reason for Our Anti-peddling Law" [Editorial], *The W.A.D. Pilot*, Jan./Feb. 1957.

15. "Deaf Solicitations are Illegal," *Glendale California News Press*, 20 February 1976, 5; "Woman Is Fined $100 on Charge of Begging," *Virginia Minnesota Mesabi News*, 13 February 1956.

slim, at best. Virtually nothing has been written on the topic of deaf peddlers, much less anything written *by* deaf peddlers. Until now, Bud Long was the only deaf peddler who had attempted to write about his experiences.

In *Everything About Deaf Peddlers*, for example, Long described a young deaf man in his thirties, possibly retarded, whose parents were thrilled to be approached by a peddler organizer who offered to teach their son how to make a living. "Had it not been for peddling," he stated, "many deaf persons would have become a burden to the taxpayers."[16] Yet Long's brief works don't provide much detail about his experiences or his perspective on peddling.

A more scholarly treatment of peddling appeared in 1980. In his article, "Deviance Within a Disabled Community: Peddling Among the Deaf," Paul Higgins identified money as the main motivator behind deaf peddling, with earnings from peddling higher than incomes associated with entry-level positions, especially for those with a high school education or less. Often, he stated, income from peddling is even greater than income from jobs that require a college degree.[17]

∞

Among the deaf people who use American Sign Language (ASL) as their primary mode of communication,

---

16. Bud Long, *Everything About Deaf Peddlers* (Dallas: Gluxit Press, 1978) and *Any Price You Wish* (Dallas: Author, 1979), 16.
17. Higgins, *Outsiders in a Hearing World*, 104–5.

there is a strong bond and sense of community. For the most part, deaf people prefer to be called deaf. Some don't mind the term "hearing impaired," but many more are offended by the view that they are impaired, as if they are less-than-whole or need to be fixed. For the most part, deaf people view deafness as the source of a different worldview, and consider themselves culturally Deaf. Members of the Deaf community share and appreciate the ability to communicate freely with one another, and they look forward to opportunities to get together at deaf clubs, sporting events, conventions, festivals, and school reunions. Many deaf people don't think twice about traveling for hours to spend an evening with deaf friends in another state.

To study the Deaf community's perception of peddling, Higgins interviewed seventy-five deaf people, their friends, and their counselors. He discovered a surprising view toward organized peddling: relief. He quoted a vocational counselor for the deaf as saying: "Now take it from me, I'm in the field of vocational rehabilitation. Some of the kids they [a deaf peddling organization] recruit are multiply handicapped [by which he meant of low intelligence, not physically handicapped]. To be perfectly honest with you, I'd have a hell of a time placing them. So this is getting them off the street."[18]

---

18. See Robert Buchanan, *Illusions of Equality: Deaf Americans in School and Factory, 1850–1950* (Washington, D.C.: Gallaudet University Press, 1999).

Higgins noted that the Deaf community is still opposed to deaf peddling, although reactions range from disgust to a lack of concern. He cited the community's negative responses, including formal denunciation and shunning of deaf peddlers. Peddling, he found, maintains a "symbolic boundary" between deaf and hearing people by increasing the stigma against deaf people, spoiling the identity of deaf people within mainstream society, and stereotyping all deaf people as helpless."[19]

Today, deaf people have many more opportunities. Therefore, the otherwise close-knit Deaf community generally views deaf peddlers with contempt. Many in the Deaf community resent the presence of deaf peddlers and see their peddling as working against the best interests of the community as a whole.

Deaf peddlers, on the other hand, look at deaf people and see only their daily struggle to prove themselves, to compensate for their deafness in a hearing world. My friends and I took pride in using our deafness to make a lot of money, and went home feeling well compensated. Although peddling requires guts, aggressiveness, and the ability to cope with public humiliation, it is an easy way to make a fairly decent living.

Occasionally, potential customers become angry. Deaf or hearing people who know ASL might say, "Get a job. Go to vocational rehab." But the vast majority

---

19. Higgins, *Outsiders in a Hearing World*, 104–5.

simply don't know any better. And the peddler, pocketing another two dollars, continues on his or her way.

Despite the recent gains made by deaf people, there are still many hearing people who cast deaf people into the old stereotypes. It is an incongruity that a deaf peddler's financial success depends on the hearing person's assumption that deaf people cannot succeed, that they need to be pitied. This psychological positioning of deaf people in a hearing culture plays an important role in understanding deaf peddling and in understanding the paradox in which deaf peddlers often find themselves.

# CHAPTER TWO

# My Story

My parents are hearing. They are hardworking midwesterners with high moral standards. My mother is a registered nurse, my father was in the military before taking a civilian job at Wright Patterson Air Force Base. I am the fourth child of five. We were all born and raised in Ohio. My three older siblings—Brian, Pamela, and Melissa—are hearing. Although my deafness is genetic, only my younger brother, Mark, and I are deaf.

In 1967, when I was six years old, a sixty-nine acre farm down the road went up for sale. My father decided to buy the land and take up farming as a second job. After we moved to the farm, Mark and I attended a deaf program housed in a public school setting. There were small classes for deaf students, and the entire school was strictly oral: only speech and voice were used, no signing was allowed. I got in trouble a lot in this program and didn't learn very much.

In 1971 my parents placed us at St. Rita School for the Deaf in Cincinnati. They had been learning more about deaf education, and thought that St. Rita would improve our communication skills and provide us with more challenging classes. Our new school used Total Communication—in other words, you communicated using any methods necessary, including American Sign Language, gestures, and spoken English. Like many deaf children who attend residential schools, we lived in a school dorm during the week and came home on weekends.

My parents have always communicated with me using the oral method because I speechread well. Mark, however, is not a good speechreader. He has always used his own method of gestures with me, our parents, and our siblings; I often act as an interpreter. After I moved away, my parents were forced to become more fluent in Mark's homemade signs.

Growing up on the farm, I loved to work hard and enjoyed every chore—yard work, driving a tractor, planting the soy beans, corn, and hay. Often, at ten or eleven at night, my father would have to call me in from the field by flashing the floodlight from the porch. I took pleasure in farming and never minded any of the hard physical labor necessary to keep the farm running. Even cleaning out the manure in the horse stalls wasn't something I balked at.

But farming wasn't the only type of work I enjoyed. I was hired for my first job when I was eleven years old. I mowed a neighbor's five-acre lawn with an old fashioned push mower. I did it in record time, too, and I kept that job for five years.

The summer of 1978, following my junior year of

high school, I went to work at Morgan Steel Company. I was a custodian, cleaning the floors and the greasy machines. I also cut the grass. My wage was $3.10 an hour.

I was a student at St. Rita until 1979. I maintained high grades and loved playing sports during those years. Despite my academic and athletic talents, I had trouble, especially as I got older, following the strict rules set by the priests and nuns. Because of my academic standing, they seemed to expect me to act as a role model. After I was caught venturing into restricted areas with a girlfriend and experimenting with marijuana, I was expelled in December of my senior year.

I transferred to Catholic Central High School, which my older brother and sisters attended, to finish out the year. I joined the track team and started aggressively looking for a summer job, since I planned to attend Gallaudet College (now, Gallaudet University) in the fall. Catholic Central had no interpreters at all, but I still managed to graduate thirteenth out of 139 hearing students, with a grade point average of 94.5.

By late spring, my job search took me to the Evans Potato Company, where I applied for a custodial position. The personnel office kept telling me to come back the next day, saying they weren't sure when a position would be available. After an entire week of showing up daily to ask about work, I was hired. They must have admired my persistence. I averaged eighty-five to ninety hours a week at Evans that entire summer, including seven hours every Saturday. My hourly salary was $3.10 with no overtime pay.

∞

Seemingly insignificant things can lead to a chain of events that drastically alter one's life. In my case, it was a love of motorcycles that eventually led me along a path I never imagined I would follow.

I was eleven years old when I first developed my fascination with motorcycles. I constantly asked my father if I could have one, and he was always reluctant. His usual comment was, "Gee, I don't know, Dennis . . . they can be dangerous." But even at that age, I had already learned never to take no for an answer easily, so I persisted. I was constantly explaining to him that there was nothing much to do there in farm country, always trying to convince him that with all those open fields and rolling hills it was a perfectly safe place to ride a motorcycle. Of course, in my mind I was imagining myself zooming up hills and jumping the river.

Mark was as enthusiastic as I, and we kept at our dad until we finally convinced him it was a good idea. He insisted we start out with a minibike, and while it wasn't exactly what we'd pictured, we hoped we could work our way up to bigger and bigger bikes as we got older.

From the first moment we got that bike, we spent all our free time riding. We became daredevils, challenging each other constantly. "Hey, Mark," I'd say, "bet I can jump it over that big hill." And he'd say, "Naaaah. No way. You can't do it." And then, of course, I'd prove to him I could.

Time went by and we became more skilled. Finally, in 1980, we moved up to a road bike. That was the summer before I entered Gallaudet, and during those last few months at home I came up with an idea. I told my father I wanted to go off on the bike and take a week's vacation. Once again, he was reluctant. He thought nineteen was too young for that kind of independence, and all I could counter with was, "Ah c'mon, Dad. It'll be my only chance before I go off to school. It'll be great!" We went back and forth about it until finally he relented.

I ended up riding the bike to Rochester, New York, to visit a friend, and it was a great trip, exactly what I'd imagined it would be. My friend and I had a great time, hanging out and talking. Out of curiosity, I decided to keep track of my mileage and gas expenses. When I arrived home and tallied them up, I discovered I'd covered 2,000 miles and spent only $30 on gasoline. When I told my father, he was incredulous. It seemed to finally convince him that riding a motorcycle was indeed a great way to travel.

When it was time for me to head off to Gallaudet, I begged my dad to let me take the motorcycle with me. He decided that first I had to prove myself and show I could keep my grades up through that first semester. Now, I'd always been a straight-A student, so his caution seemed a little silly. Wasn't it obvious that my academic achievement was the one thing he didn't have to worry about? Still, I knew there was only one way I was going to get what I wanted. So we had a deal.

∞

When I started at Gallaudet, I was excited about the possibility of playing on the football team. Unfortunately, the team folded that fall for lack of players, a real disappointment. I'd been looking forward to being part of the team and now I had to find something else to do. I decided on weight training, with the idea of building myself up for a renewed football team the following fall. At six feet tall and 175 pounds, I could benefit from putting on some muscle mass. My goal was to lift my way up to 200 pounds.

I was paying for much of my tuition and living expenses, and at first I received $300 a month from Supplemental Security Income (SSI). The benefits follow strict guidelines based on one's assets and salary. Anything I earned was a sensitive issue. The SSI program required me to report any earnings over $75 a month so that my benefit could be recalculated. Every month, I filled out a form providing details of my earnings and stating why I felt I should continue with the program. Overall, the SSI program was quite a hassle.

But I did want to earn money, so I decided to cancel SSI. I took a part-time job in the university's tutoring center helping students with math, computer programming, and science. After I started tutoring, one of the center's staff members asked if I'd like to do some work on his farm during my free time. Then his partner, who worked at a collection agency in Virginia, recruited me to be a full-time file clerk. Altogether, during my freshman year I worked forty to fifty hours a week, in addition to my academic load.

I dove into my studies, and received the highest score on the first test in my pre-calculus class. I was curious about who had received the second highest score, and found out it was someone named Rafael. I introduced myself, and we quickly became good friends.

Rafael had been accepted to the university after his junior year in high school, which is very impressive. He was from Puerto Rico, and he spoke both Spanish and English, but he knew nothing about sign language. He was a very easy person to get along with. We challenged each other on pre-calculus problems and we made a great team. As the year went along, we both decided we wanted to major in engineering. Rafael and I had a lot in common, and by the second semester we were roommates.

During that first semester, I kept my deal with my dad by achieving a 4.0 average, even tutoring somebody in my pre-calculus class where I had met Rafael. Shortly after the first test, a guy named Don approached me and asked for my help, so I helped him throughout the semester. Glad to see me doing so well, my father agreed to fulfill his part of the bargain. There was only one problem. I found I really didn't want to bring my old motorcycle back to Gallaudet. I told my dad I wanted a newer, better bike.

While he was thinking about it, I reminded him

about that 2,000-mile trip, the one that only cost $30 in gas money, and after some discussion, which included Mark's input as well, Dad decided to buy not just one new bike, but three! One for me, one for Mark, and one for himself. They were Honda 400cc Nighthawks, regular bikes, but brand new.

I took a Greyhound bus home for spring break, and I still remember getting off the bus and seeing those bright, shiny new motorcycles. They were incredible. Mine was all black, and it was perfect. I insisted on riding it back to school when break was over, an idea my father wasn't exactly crazy about. Especially since the temperature outside was just below freezing, thirty degrees.

It was an eight-hour trip from Ohio to Washington, D.C., and although thirty degrees isn't terribly cold, when you're riding a motorcycle and have to take the wind chill factor into consideration, it's *very* cold! I bundled up in a snowmobile suit, said good-bye to my folks, and nearly froze to death. I kept stopping for hot chocolate along the way, but it would warm me up only for a while. Still, when I finally arrived back in D.C., I stood out in the frosty parking lot and gazed at my new bike, admiring its newness and the freedom it represented. Cars had always seemed too confining, they made me feel hemmed in and restless. But the bike— now that was a whole different experience!

So there I was, a guy with a motorcycle at Gallaudet. My classes usually ended at about four in the afternoon, and as soon as my last class was finished I'd get on the bike and head out to more open areas around D.C. Sometimes I'd ride until ten at night, then come back and study until two in the morning. Riding was my escape, a way of finding a little release, a perfect stress reducer.

Rafael hadn't seen much of the United States. So after spring break, I asked him if he'd like to join me on a weekend road trip to Rochester. He had a brother who lived in Buffalo and asked if I'd mind including a visit there. I was happy to have company, happy to share my passion for riding with a buddy. There were only two things I wanted to make sure of: one, that Rafael didn't mind wearing a helmet; and two, that he had no trepidation at the prospect of riding on the back of a motorcycle. He was fine with both. So on April 3, we finished our classes at four in the afternoon and made our preparations for the trip. It was still cold out, so we bundled up in warm clothes, put on our helmets and left campus around five o'clock.

To get to Rochester we took the highway up through Pennsylvania. The highway passes through mountains and the scenery was glorious. We were both enjoying the ride immensely. By nine that night, we were getting hungry, so we stopped to eat at a McDonald's, then bundled up again and got back on the road. The highway continued to twist and turn through the mountains, and even though it was dark, I was still enjoying being out there.

Then we came to an S-curve in the road with a sign

that read "35 MPH." Normally, I might have scoffed at that speed reduction. That night though, for whatever reason, I slowed down. As we were coming around the curve, a car in the oncoming lane had its high-beam headlights on. They were blinding. I flashed my own headlights to remind the other driver that his brights were on, but it was already too late. It was as if I had developed a blind spot. In the second it took to regain my vision, I realized my bike had drifted into the other lane. There was no time to swerve away. The other driver hit his brakes just before we crashed.

It all happened so fast. My motorcycle was off in the trees somewhere and I was lying on the ground. I felt absolutely no pain—just very strange, as if I were dreaming. I remember wondering how I'd ended up on the ground, remember two people standing over me looking down, remember wondering what exactly had happened. Then I recalled leaving Gallaudet to go to Rochester to see my friend, and suddenly I knew I'd crashed the motorcycle. I looked over and saw Rafael lying next to me, unconscious. I was very scared. I reached over and shook his face. When he didn't wake up, I thought he was dead.

By then, people were talking to me, but I didn't understand what they were saying. I began to notice that my back felt funny, numb . . . the kind of feeling you might get in your arm when it falls asleep.

When the ambulance arrived, I struggled to stand up, but I couldn't, which puzzled me. The paramedics restrained me, then immobilized my head and neck and lifted me very carefully into the ambulance. I asked about Rafael and they told me not to worry.

During the ride to the hospital, I suddenly got a strange burning sensation in my back. It felt very hot, and so strange that I passed out. When I came to again, I was in the emergency room. I could see that someone had drawn dashed lines across my chest with red and blue markers, though I couldn't figure out why. I looked down at my feet and was surprised to see a doctor poking my toes with a pin. He looked at me, and I speechread his words, "Do you feel this?"

"Nah," I answered, "do it deeper."

He poked my toes again. Nothing. Then he moved up and poked the pin into my shoulder. That hurt, and I reacted sharply. He went back to my feet and worked his way up my legs, poking to see where sensation, if any, began. By this time, I was greatly concerned and tried to convey this to the doctor by giving him worried looks. He said they'd have to take an X ray in order to figure out what was wrong. After that, I fell asleep for a while and when I woke up again I was in the intensive care unit.

The accident had occurred at 9:30 that night, but it wasn't until 2 A.M. that they finally called my parents. I know they didn't give them all the details, only that I had been in an accident and was in ICU. My parents later told me they were frantic with worry. They immediately woke Mark and set out on the eight-hour drive from Ohio to Pennsylvania. I think about them going on that trip, with little information except that their son was seriously injured, and realize how awful it must have been for them.

I remember waking up and seeing their faces, feeling relief, fear, and love. I cried. I asked about Rafael and learned that he was not dead, but gravely injured and in a coma.

"You're gonna be okay," my dad kept saying, "you're gonna be okay, son. It's okay now."

I lay there watching my parents discuss my case with the doctor and noticed pain in my back for the first time.

My parents stayed by my side, asking if I could be transferred to a hospital in Ohio, and three days after the accident I was flown by hospital plane to St. Anthony's Hospital in Columbus. Once there, I spent a week lying on a "sandwich bed," being flipped over every four hours to prevent bed sores.

It's hard to describe what that was like, lying there for days on end. Time became a surreal thing, so slow it felt almost suspended. I thought about Rafael recuperating in a different hospital in Pittsburgh. He'd had to have his left leg amputated above the knee. His left hand was paralyzed, his left eye dislocated, and he'd suffered a ruptured spleen. I'd called him via TTY after he came out of his coma to say I was sorry about the accident. He had little to say, except to answer my questions with a "toneless" yes or no.

On April 15, I underwent four hours of surgery to correct my vertebrae, one of which was completely misaligned. Once it was back in position, the surgeons set a stainless steel Harrington rod on each side of my spinal column to keep it stable. When I began to come out of the anesthetic, I opened my eyes long enough to see a nurse; he smiled and gave me a "thumbs up." I drifted off to sleep again, assuming his gesture meant I would walk again.

When I woke up several hours later, the one thing I was aware of was pain. It felt as if my spinal cord was being squeezed very hard. When I complained, I was given morphine and the pain disappeared, at least for a while.

"Do you feel anything in your legs?" That's the question the doctors kept asking. And my answer was always, "No." I didn't understand why I wasn't getting better. I'd thought the surgery would fix the problem, that the "thumbs up" meant I'd be fine again. I began to doubt everything. And when I asked the doctor about my legs, all he did was raise one finger and mouth the word, "Wait." I waited. And when I asked again, he said, "Give it a little more time."

Finally, I forced him to level with me. I'll never forget his words and what they looked like on his lips. He held up one finger and said, "One percent chance you will walk again."

One percent? I was shocked, couldn't speak. It felt as if I was coming apart, as if my whole life had been obliterated, cancelled. All the things I loved to do passed through my mind—football, walking, sports, working on the farm. Then I thought of all the things I'd hoped for in the future—love, marriage, fatherhood. All of that was gone? I couldn't imagine a life without those things.

When I was finally able to ask the doctor why the chances were so grim, he explained that my spinal cord had been bruised and permanently damaged. I was permanently paralyzed from the chest down.

To say I was devastated is an understatement. I cried for hours, feeling my life was over. I was twenty years old and everything I had envisioned, all my dreams, seemed to vanish like dust. I can't be with a woman, I can't play football, I can't farm . . . can't, can't, can't. I was engulfed in grief and loss and could not even begin to imagine a way out.

As I lay in bed wondering what was ahead, wondering what kind of life I'd have, there was an overwhelming grief deep inside me that no one could talk me out of. Not my mom and dad who visited me every day. Not the doctors or the nurses. It was pure hell, and I woke up every morning wishing I were dead.

In May, after I healed from the surgery, I was transferred to a rehabilitation center at Ohio State University in Columbus. When I arrived there, the doctor's first words were, "You have a long way to go." He was about forty-five years old, very cautious and strict as he explained that the program included not only physical work, but emotional and psychological adjustment as well. He said it was going to take a while.

"But I'm planning to go back to Gallaudet in the fall," I told him, and we argued back and forth about that possibility. I couldn't imagine that it was going to take more than a few months before I could leave. And he was just as adamant that it was going to take a year or longer.

When an orderly from physical therapy showed up and said, "Come on, let's go exercise," all I did was shoo him away. But he kept harassing me until finally, partly out of frustration, I consented to let him take me down to try some kind of exercise. I'd been lying in bed now for over a month, and it was tremendously difficult just to have to sit up in a wheelchair. I was dizzy and overly sensitive, plus I still had tremendous pain. They'd switched me from morphine to the less addictive, and less effective, codeine. I was having trouble sleeping, and staying in one position for any length of time at all was impossible. I was beginning to wonder if pain would always be a part of my life.

For my first physical therapy session, the therapist carried over some one-pound weights, and I remember saying to myself, "She's got to be kidding! I used to lift 250 pounds!" She was a young woman in her thirties with a very positive attitude, and I remember her urging, "Just try it. If we need to increase the weight, we can." But when I took the weight, I couldn't lift it at all. My muscles had atrophied, all my strength was gone. I was starting all over again from square one, just like a baby. I had to learn how to do simple tasks in new ways, to swallow my pride and accept things the way they were.

And it wasn't easy. In occupational therapy, I had to

sit in front of a pegboard with rows of pegs at four different heights, and place rings of various colors on the pegs. It was a test of my ability to reach, and I remember thinking the first time, *Oh brother, baby stuff.* But I found myself placing the rings on even the lowest row with extreme difficulty. Looking up at the top row, I wondered if I would ever get to that level!

The doctor had been right. I did have a long way to go. But remembering his words kept me working. I decided I had to prove him wrong, despite the debilitating pain in my back.

One of my roommates at the rehab center was a guy named Tom Lowry. I first met him when I noticed him following the pretty nurses around the halls. When he caught me grinning at him, he came over and shook my hand, telling me I could do the same thing. I thought he was joking but later realized it was one of his favorite pastimes!

Tom was a young man about my age who had been injured in a construction accident five months ago. His back had gotten smashed by a mobile home he was trying to fix; somehow the iron support bar broke and the trailer crashed down with him underneath. He was paralyzed from the waist down.

We got along great. When I was still reluctant to try physical therapy, Tom would come over and gesture, "Come on! Exercise!" He was only trying to be supportive and encouraging, but I kept putting him off—it was tough to respond with enthusiasm as long as I was suffering so much pain.

Another one of my mentors while I was at rehab was Father Colby Grimes. He had been one of the teachers at St. Rita and when he heard about my accident, he volunteered to help me every day for two months. He knew American Sign Language, and came most every afternoon and evening to spend time with me. Tom and my other roommates talked to me using Father Grimes as an interpreter.

Then the seemingly impossible happened. I woke up one morning with no pain at all! The doctor had told me I might have pain for the rest of my life, but it had disappeared just as if someone had flicked a switch. I could barely believe it was gone, and for a long time I worried that the same switch might turn back on again.

Once my pain was gone, Tom became my workout buddy. He teased me in the beginning when I could only lift 5 pounds. He could lift 100. But competing with Tom spurred me on and made me put all my effort into my workouts.

I gradually became stronger and began to feel better. Tom and I began to have wheelchair races in the hallway on our way to physical therapy. There was a system of underground tunnels that connected the rehab center to the hospital and we used to race along those tunnels incredibly fast. There were some upward slopes, and I remember my arms working hard enough to make my chest heave and sweat pour down my forehead. Our races helped enormously to build up my endurance, and gradually I found myself working up the scale, able to lift 60, then 80, then finally 100 pounds.

Tom and I always bragged back and forth, and one of the orderlies in the physical therapy room joined in. He was a big guy, we thought he was cool, and he pointed to Tom one day and said to me, "He told me you're nothing!"

Of course, this got me going. "What?" I said, "I'm much better than him."

"Oh yeah," he replied, "then prove it. Let me see how good you are."

We sat side by side, Tom and I, and started lifting. We got up to 170 pounds, 180, and finally I beat Tom by lifting 200 pounds.

My doctor, ever cautious, became quite concerned when he saw I was ahead in my rehab schedule. He thought I might be skipping stages and made me show him exactly what I could do. After that, he had to admit I was doing a great job, better than he'd ever suspected was possible.

Tom and I used to visit other patients at the center, and I discovered a lot of people who were worse off than I . . . people in constant pain, a man with muscular dystrophy, a man in a wheelchair who did nothing but stare at the walls all day. I began to think I was relatively lucky—I had strong arms, I could get myself around and take care of myself—I began to realize how important attitude is to the rehabilitation process.

Around the middle of June, I asked my doctor how I was doing and if he thought I'd be back at Gallaudet in the fall. He said I was doing well, but told me that the hole in my leg had still not healed well enough for me to be able to leave. My first reaction was disappointment, but then decided I just had to do something to change his prognosis. I stepped up my workouts, learned to drive a car with hand controls, and figured out how to cook from my wheelchair. I used to pass out brownies to the staff and the other patients, and people weren't just amazed by the change in my abilities, but by the change in my attitude as well.

Of course, the biggest thing I had to thank for those changes was finally being free of pain. I felt I could do anything, it was like being on a high. In early July, Tom went home after spending nearly a year in rehab. I missed him terribly, but I knew it was important to keep a positive attitude. A week later, the doctor came in and said, "You're discharged. Go home." It was July 15, a little more than three months since my accident.

He went on to tell me I'd had the fastest recovery he'd ever seen. The average stay was six to twelve months, so apparently he didn't quite trust my accelerated progress. He advised my parents to keep me home for a year, stressing the emotional and psychological healing I still had to undergo. He expected me to have a difficult adjustment to a nondisabled world. My parents mentioned his suggestion, and I responded with a vehement "No!" After some discussion, they gave in and let me make plans for returning to school.

Those plans included a car with hand controls. I needed transportation in order to get to my file clerk job in Virginia. I'd asked my boss to hold it open for me when I'd talked to him shortly after my accident, and he'd promised he would. He was a great boss and a good signer, and I didn't want to disappoint him.

"Can't you take the bus?" my father asked.

"No," I answered, "they're not wheelchair accessible." This was mostly true. Although some buses in D.C. were accessible at that time, it still would have taken forever to get to doctor's appointments and my job, which was twenty miles away from the Gallaudet campus. So we ended up purchasing a big used car and having it fitted with hand controls.

I set off for Gallaudet with my doctor's final words to me in my mind. "Be careful when you go back, it will be harder than you think." I'd told him I'd deal with it.

My parents followed me in their car on my trip back to D.C., worried that I had less than three weeks' practice driving the new car. But the drive went smoothly and it felt good to be back on campus. Gallaudet is a small school, and after just my freshman year I knew most of the students at least by face, if not by name. Many of them, even a few people I barely knew, welcomed me back and expressed their concern. All of a sudden, I felt as if I were drowning in their kindness. I choked up, remembering the last time I'd been at Gallaudet.

I couldn't get the image of myself walking around campus out of my mind, and the dissonance between my old life and this new one seemed suddenly overwhelming. I tried to keep my feelings in check, tried to stay positive. I thought about how I'd loved to play football, and wheeled myself over to the field where I'd

played with my not-so-motivated teammates the previ-
ous fall. It turned out the team was practicing, and one
of the players who'd known me before the accident
broke away and came over.

"How're you doing?" he asked.

"Hi . . . okay, fine," I answered, but I was fighting
back tears.

The doctor had been right. This was harder than I'd
ever imagined. I didn't have Tom there to support me. I
felt completely alone.

Then, to make things worse, my friend from the
team called the other players over. He introduced me to
them by saying, "This guy was on our team last year. He
was a good player, really loves football, really has the
heart for the game."

His words made me terribly uncomfortable and
only underscored the huge loss I had experienced. I
managed to thank him for his kindness, but all I wanted
was to end the situation as quickly as possible. I told
them I had to go and most of them went back to their
practice. My friend walked with me for a while. He'd
noticed my reaction and wanted to know why I was upset. I explained that since my accident, this was my first
confrontation with my former life, with the things I
used to be able to do. And that it was my first real expo-
sure as a person in a wheelchair to people who remembered me differently. He seemed to understand, but
that still didn't make things easier. With one such meeting over with, there were many more left to go.

Seventeen years later, it's still not easy to tell this

story. It makes me remember and even re-experience the tremendous loss and adjustment I faced. On the other hand, it makes me proud that I got through it and that I'm the same person I was before the accident in terms of personality, perseverance, and temperament . . . although there are some things about me that did change. Before my accident, I think I knew very little about the capacity of the human heart, especially mine, to bear up under adversity. I know I've learned to be positive and resourceful, and I feel fortunate that my life continues to unfold in a way that is rich with people and self-discovery.

# CHAPTER THREE

# Early Days on the Road

As the doctor predicted, my first few months back at Gallaudet were difficult. Everything was new because I had to learn ways to accommodate my disability. I lost all of my friends from the year before, especially the football players—we just ran out of things to talk about, we didn't seem to have anything in common anymore.

I worked full-time for the collection agency in Virginia the first two years, and took a full courseload as well. It was physically and mentally exhausting. In 1983, I decided to take a short break in my studies and accepted a one-semester internship at IBM.

Slowly, I figured out ways to compensate for being paralyzed. I started going out, being more active socially, and even began dating again. It was wonderful to realize I could get back into the swing of things. I often thought of Rafael, who'd finally left the hospital and gone back to Puerto Rico to be with his family. His parents had planned to sue me for his injuries, but he wouldn't let them. I wondered if his life was knitting back together, as mine was.

By the end of the fall semester, I was ready to start studying again. I registered for classes for spring, and was browsing through the campus bookstore when I ran into an old acquaintance. I had tutored Don in pre-calculus my freshman year, but we hadn't seen each other since the accident. He was looking for a room-mate for the spring semester, and I readily agreed. Don was a lot of fun and we had always enjoyed one other's company. Because of my disability, we were assigned to a newly renovated dorm, in a large room with a private bathroom.

As Don was unpacking his things the day we moved in, I noticed his peddling cards. I had never seen peddling cards before and, for that matter, I had never even heard of deaf peddling. When I asked about them, he told me what they were for and explained how he peddled. He said he made a good deal of money selling his pamphlets. "They go like crazy!" he said, telling me that on good days he could earn $170 in four hours.

Looking at his pamphlet (shown in figure 1), I found that hard to believe. It was nothing more than a small yellow brochure with an eagle and a flag imprinted on the cover, with the message, "Hello! I am a deaf person. I am selling this Deaf Education System Book to support my college expenses. Would you kindly buy one? Pay any price you wish! Thank you for your donation!" The inside pages illustrated the manual alphabet and some basic signs. On the final inside page was a list of suggestions for learning sign language. *Don must be nuts*, I thought, *to think he could make money off such an*

**Hello!**

I AM A
DEAF PERSON

I am selling this
## Deaf
## Education System
Book to support my
college expenses.

Will   You   Kindly   Buy   One?

Pay Any Price You Wish!

**THANK YOU!
FOR DONATION**

*Figure 1*

*item*. But then he did always seem to be jetting off here
and there, despite the fact he didn't have a regular job.
Despite his enthusiasm, I quickly forgot all about this
sideline of his.

We were a great duo, Don and I. At that point I was
working full time as a data specialist in addition to attending school and interning at IBM. I liked to work
and I liked making money. Don must have decided I
had what it takes to be a good business partner, and be-

fore long we launched our first business venture. We
spent $2,000 on a 52-inch television with a caption de-
coder, something quite unusual on campus at that time,
and started hosting an all-night movie fest on Friday
nights. We charged each student three dollars and offered soda and free popcorn. It was immensely successful, and we ended up making $400 the first night alone.

Any business conducted on campus had to be a
college-related promotion, so we entered into an agree-
ment with the basketball coach, giving half our earnings to the Gallaudet basketball fund. After this first
success, we decided to host a Super Bowl event using
our new TV, and later bought a camcorder and video-
taped students. We gave out ticket stubs inviting them
to come and watch "their show" for five dollars. Every
plan we made seemed to make more money than the
last, and we quickly realized that these were only the
first of many joint business ventures to come.

Don had to leave Gallaudet in the middle of the fall
1994 semester. He moved back to his home in Ocala,
Florida with his grandmother and mother. I missed
him, but we continued to keep in touch.

I knew it was important to have a great deal of experience in the field before getting a permanent job, so I decided to get as much work experience as possible. I was
one of the university's top students, and in the spring I
began interviewing for a summer internship. An AT&T
recruiter came to campus to interview the university's
top ten computer science students, and asked me to in-

tern for the company's information systems division. So I moved out to Denver, with all travel expenses taken care of by the company.

In Colorado I lived in an apartment with one roommate. I didn't know anybody, and it was pretty lonely. Although it was a paid internship, I still needed to earn some extra money. Then I remembered Don and his peddling cards. I called and asked him to send me one of his cards. When the sample card arrived, I took it to a local print shop and for only $125 they printed up a thousand copies.

Now that I had made an investment, I asked Don how to proceed. It sounded easy when he explained it to me via TTY.

"Just pass the cards around," he said, "then people will give you money."

It turned out to be easier said than done, although I did earn the first two dollars easily—but only because the people at the print shop wanted to buy one of the cards they had just printed!

After that first sale, it was all uphill. I went to a mall and wasn't particularly successful. I only made one dollar after an hour of peddling. So I called Don again and complained about my bad luck. He agreed to come through Denver on his way to the Deaf World Games in Los Angeles.

Soon after he arrived, he took me along to watch him peddle at a nearby McDonald's. His method was to swiftly pass out a card to each customer, then circulate again in a few minutes and pick up money. In five minutes he made $15. He instructed, "Have some guts, go into a restaurant, pass out the cards, collect the money, get out, and then go to another restaurant and do it all over again!" Simple.

Don had to continue on to California, so I soon found myself on my own again. It was easy, though, to remember his coaching. My first stop was a cafeteria-style restaurant. I followed Don's advice and made $38 in the first thirty minutes. I was amazed.

The next day, a Saturday, I went to the Crossroads Mall in Boulder and peddled for eight hours. I earned $280 and I was not only amazed, I was hooked.

I tried to come up with an even better area to peddle, and realized the best place would be one where the customer base changed regularly over a period of several hours. The airport! Four hours peddling there the next day earned me $300.

I'd always worked full time while I was a student at Gallaudet—that was the only way I knew how to make money. But now I'd discovered another way, and when I went back to school for my senior year, I peddled on weekends for my living expenses.

❧

By the spring of 1986, graduation was approaching. I received several job offers but turned them all down—Don and I had made other plans. We were going to work together as a team, peddling across the country and making big money. He was waiting for me in Florida, so I headed south as soon as graduation was over. I owned a full-sized van, and we planned to live out of it as we traveled. But things didn't quite turn out that way.

Once I arrived in Florida I discovered that Don had acquired a new girlfriend. He no longer wanted to go on the road. After looking forward to this trip for a long time and turning down three solid job offers, all with good pay, I was being informed that the whole thing was off. Just like that. You might say I was upset, although freaked out would be a more accurate description! Don's change of heart felt exactly like a punch in the face.

I stayed in Florida for a while, getting used to the change of plans and figuring out what I wanted to do with myself. While I was there, Don introduced me to Social Security Disability Insurance (SSDI). As a deaf person, I was apparently automatically eligible for SSDI.

Don explained that people who apply for Social Security benefits are always asked, "Do you want to apply for SSI?" Many applicants learn through the grapevine to enter "no," so they will then be considered as applicants for SSDI. The program isn't as strict as SSI and it usually provides a higher benefit. I had never learned about SSDI, and had always just checked the box for SSI, not knowing I was missing the opportunity to get higher benefits.

I was eligible for quite a nice benefit because I had worked a great deal during college, and SSDI benefits are based on what one has paid into the system and on one's salary at the last place of employment. Some may consider it unfair that deaf people who are able to work can receive Social Security benefits, but the fact is that the government labels deafness as a "disability," and deaf people are legally entitled to them.

Of course, the SSDI program includes other disabilities, but the label "deaf" carries power in the SSDI system. It almost always assures instant access to benefits. All that is required is an audiogram to prove that one is deaf. For some reason, an individual in a wheelchair is subject to far more evaluation, documentation, and red tape to determine if a real handicap to employment is present. When I first learned about the Social Security system, I was surprised at the "respect" being labeled deaf provoked. (At least in the government's eyes!)

The SSDI program sounded ideal, and I was soon receiving about $600 each month, double what I had received on SSI before I started working. Although I recognized how addictive that kind of income can be, it seemed like free money! I remember asking myself, why work? But I had always worked, and I wasn't about to stop.

In June, I was anxious to get going. I decided to peddle on my own, leaving Don to the bliss of his newfound love. I set off eagerly towards New Orleans, planning to travel and peddle for a while before working on my master's degree.

Some independent deaf peddlers starting out are lucky enough to get advice from more experienced peddlers, who can help them avoid wasting their time and their effort. I wasn't fortunate enough to have a mentor, and began my peddling career in a pretty disorganized manner. I was weary most of the time from the constant travel and from sleeping in the van in all kinds of weather, including some nights when I had to plug in a space heater just to keep warm.

Because I had no training and no real mentor, I did things the hard way. I traveled like crazy, jumping around to different places willy-nilly. I occasionally left the airport to try my luck in a different environment. Small towns are often a good choice because the people there are friendlier and less sophisticated, more apt to make a purchase. Still, even with prior experience, it would be difficult to know how long I could work there. Perhaps a manager of a restaurant might begin to recognize me after a week or two and report my presence. Or the police themselves might notice me. Police attitudes vary considerably. Some will escort you straight to jail. Others will simply ask you to move on. In either case, you're back on the road.

One of the first things I learned is that to be successful, a peddler has to keep track of all the locations he or she has worked—which were successful, which were not, what the earnings were and how they varied at specific times and places. Many peddlers use memo books, calendars, and ledgers. Since I have a degree in computer science, I started to log this information on my computer using spreadsheet software, noting dates, locations, earnings, and hours worked.

By tracking of how much money I made at different times of the year, I learned that summer is a profitable season, with its influx of tourists. Holidays are also very good. People are in high spirits and are generally carrying extra cash in their pockets. Even the time of day makes a great difference. For example, a peddler might find the mid-morning hours poor. This might be a time for a rest. Then the midday hours, say eleven to one, might be great for business, especially near a restaurant where people are coming and going before and after lunch. In the afternoon, a university library where students are studying might be a profitable stop. Around dinner time, from five to eight, a restaurant would again be the place to go.

I quickly learned that restaurants, especially fast-food outlets, are great peddling locations. I once went into a Shoney's in Atlanta, keeping an eye out for the manager. As soon as he went into the kitchen, I circulated quickly among the tables, placing my pamphlets in front of customers. As I was making a second round to pick up money or cards, the manager came out and noticed what I was doing. He got very upset, pulled my wheelchair out of the dining area, and started pushing me toward the exit. I managed to pick up some of the money people had left on their tables on this quick trip out, and simply went on to the next restaurant once he'd pushed me out the door. For a salesman, it's always important to shake off the failures and doggedly look forward to the next opportunity.

Each deaf peddler has his or her own preference as far as location is concerned. Some peddle only in restaurants, others only in airports or bus terminals. Some peddlers decide in advance to work a set number of hours per day. Others might establish a dollar amount. Still others might take, say, one hundred cards or pamphlets and work until they're sold, hoping it will take an hour instead of an entire day. If you're lucky, customers will be in a buying mood; if you're not, it can seem as though every customer either ignores you or declines to buy.

Some peddlers prefer large public gatherings such as craft fairs, carnivals, and state fairs. I never worked those locations because of the difficulty in getting around in my wheelchair, but a friend of mine earned about $600 a day peddling at a ten-day county fair in Peoria, Illinois. Other peddlers earn great money at the Indy 500. I think even if accessibility hadn't been a problem, though, I'd still have preferred the airport, which is protected from the weather and always air conditioned in the summer!

Obviously, airports were my favorite places to peddle. Most deaf peddlers do their peddling at airports for the simple reason that the multitude of people coming and going all day guarantees sure money. Airports provide a constantly changing customer base with little chance of repeat business, as opposed to a mall, for instance, where the customer "cycle" is completed in four to six months, accompanied by a predicted drop off in sales. In addition to an ever-changing population, there is an abundance of places where one can choose to peddle . . . dozens of concourses and hundreds of gates.

But other locations are good for peddling as well. In malls, people are already out shopping and generally in a mood to spend money, which is always beneficial to a peddler's business. And a peddler learns quickly that weekends are the times to visit malls, while weekdays often aren't worth the trip. But then, as I've already mentioned earlier, malls are prone to customer-base problems; namely, you find the same local people returning week after week or month after month. They've seen the peddler's product, and sooner rather than later, the market reaches its saturation point.

Sometimes, however, just the opposite happens. Once when I was peddling at a food court in one of Atlanta's malls, I noticed a policeman watching me. After a while, he came up to me and asked what I was doing. I handed him one of my pamphlets and he got on his walkie-talkie, asking a supervisor what to do about me. Five minutes later he received a reply and told me there was no peddling allowed in the mall. "But just between you and me," he said, "you can continue for one more hour." Then he handed me two dollars and said he wished he could give me more, but that was all he had in his pocket! I worked as quickly as I could for the next hour to earn as much as possible in the time I had. It certainly was a different experience—a police officer who helped out with my daily income, rather than helping me out of the mall!

In addition to the motivation supplied by an overall goal, there is the day-to-day, minute-to-minute motivation a peddler must maintain. From experience, I know how easily frustrated one can become when selling is difficult and a day doesn't measure up to expectations. It's normal to feel disenchanted when a potential customer turns you down, but it's more important to shrug it off and look ahead to the next opportunity.

Occasionally, instead of being brushed off, a deaf peddler encounters a hearing customer who knows some sign language and is quite excited to be able to use it. Meeting someone with whom one can communicate and who has some knowledge of Deaf culture is refreshing, but it still doesn't deter a peddler from trying to make a sale.

At a Steak 'n Shake late one evening, I was making my usual rounds, putting a pamphlet on each table and heading back to retrieve what people had left, when a customer stopped to talk to me. Apparently he had recently seen the movie *Children of a Lesser God* and wanted to discuss it. We were communicating by writing back and forth, and I asked if he'd mind if I finished my rounds first. He told me to go ahead, and when I returned he offered to buy me dinner. I had to turn him down because I still had more work to do, and he told me he'd been inspired by the movie and asked if he could write me a check. I told him that would be difficult for me, and so he opened his wallet. All he had was two twenty-dollar bills and, after a moment of hesitation, he handed me both.

Time is money for a peddler, and although he or she may talk with a hearing signer for a minute or two, it mainly boils down to an exercise in good customer relations. Sooner rather than later, the peddler will say, "Need to go make money, will you buy a book?" Usually the hearing signer will respond, "Sure, I'll buy," and give the peddler extra money! It has often seemed ironic to me that people who have taken the time to learn something about Deaf culture will be so thoughtlessly compliant in a transaction that is basically damaging to deaf people and to the Deaf community.

Once I had picked up the peddling life, the travel, different sights, and new people were quite exciting. At first, I was so amazed at the amount of money and independence that I never stopped to wonder what I might be giving up. But despite the new experiences I was lonely, depressed, and worried about my lack of cash.

Then in Texas, I remembered a friend who lived in Albuquerque, New Mexico. Bud and I had grown up at the St. Rita School for the Deaf, and later we'd been good buddies at Gallaudet. I missed his easy-going, fun personality and decided to look him up over Thanksgiving weekend. Suddenly the whole trip seemed worthwhile. Bud was surprised and pleased to see me, and we spent hours catching up on each other's lives. I felt reinvigorated after visiting with Bud, and decided to continue on to California.

Don had told me about a peddler friend of his in Los Angeles, so before heading to California I gave him a call. Mike was taking advantage of the fact that one of his deaf friends in Los Angeles lived in a subsidized apartment, and the two of them were paying virtually nothing for rent. He offered to pick me up at the airport on Friday and to let me stay with them for a short time.

When I got into Mike's car, he showed me this terrific keychain he had purchased. Mike peddled at Los Angeles International Airport (LAX), and a Mexican peddler had taken him to a huge indoor flea market a few weeks before. The market was full of many different types of foreign items at a very low cost. Looking around, Mike spied a keychain that was attached to a small tool kit. The kit consisted of a small black case with a clear plastic front. It held three miniature screwdrivers, each with a different color handle—yellow, red, and green. The screwdrivers could be used for small screws on eyeglasses or watches. Although not very well made, it was a useful item, and Mike bought several cases and started selling the keychain as a novelty item.

Mike was so enthusiastic about his find that I tried peddling with it at LAX the very next day. To my surprise, I found I had never made so much money so quickly! I went back to LAX the next day, but as soon as I got there, I met a deaf Mexican peddler who told me she worked for an organized peddling ring. At the next gate, I saw another Mexican deaf peddler, and another at the next gate, and so on. There must have been ten or twenty Mexican peddlers working LAX. I would describe most of them as having "minimal language skills," meaning that even their signing skills were below average. Their appearance was rough, and a few were even ready to fight with me, defensive of their territory and antagonistic toward any potential competition.

Since negotiation seemed an unlikely avenue, I simply left Los Angeles. My next stop was San Francisco, where I encountered yet another Mexican deaf peddling ring; different peddlers, but they were selling the same novelties as those at LAX . . . obviously, this was a highly organized and very assertive peddling ring.

This was my first real experience with peddling rings, although I had heard about them earlier in my trip. A peddler organizer, or cow, generally targets deaf people who are struggling. They may be having financial troubles or vocational problems, but they almost always have a limited education. The cow also looks for loyalty, and when he finds the right combination of trouble and fidelity, he will take a deaf person under his wing. "You want to buy a car?" he'll ask. "Well, sure," comes the reply, "but how?" He'll then take the prospective peddlers to his fine home and show them the lifestyle they, too, can acquire.

Perhaps he'll set a goal for them—a new car like his—to entice them to start peddling. For a while, he'll even let them stay at his home for free. He might supply them with a used car, telling them they must prove themselves to him over a year's time. Then, he will offer to put a portion of their earnings into a "savings plan," so they can save enough to buy that brand new car. This type of arrangement is akin to an insurance policy for the cow, keeping the underlings working toward an incentive for the future.

A cow needs to be able to communicate well with different types of deaf people. He has to be good at gaining their trust and making them believe that the arrangement he is offering is a win-win proposition for both parties. In truth, the peddler may be expected to turn over all his peddling earnings, and may even be required to fulfill a specific dollar amount each day. To be sure there's no cheating, the cow might frisk him to be certain the peddler is not holding back money.

In a different arrangement, the peddler might be expected to turn over 50 to 75 percent of his weekly income (and maybe even a specified amount toward a "savings plan"), with the cow providing the room and board, plus the novelties or cards to be peddled—not to mention the very generous opportunity to work for him. The cow can earn as much as $2,000 a week from each peddler.

And where does he find these peddlers? I know one man who manages deaf peddlers. He owns his own home and is deaf, but has never actually worked as a peddler. He is very involved in the Deaf community, always attending Deaf events such as softball tournaments. The reason he's so involved is that it gives him the opportunity to meet deaf people he might then hire. It's the way cows recruit.

Although some might conclude that a peddling organizer at least offers deaf people with minimal language skills or job training a better chance at making a living, not all cows are benevolent. Any mention of deaf peddling rings wouldn't be complete without bringing up an infamous case from 1997. State and federal agents raided two apartments in Queens, New York, that summer. They discovered fifty-seven deaf, illegal Mexican immigrants living in two apartments, along with seven people who were reported to be the ringleaders.

The cows, who included both hearing and deaf people, had smuggled the peddlers into Los Angeles with false immigration papers. Once in the United States, the peddlers were transported to New York City, where they were forced each day to go into the subway system to peddle key chains and other trinkets. They were living in squalid conditions and given minimal money for food and transportation. Their immigration papers had been confiscated by the cows, and few of them were literate in Spanish, let alone English or American Sign Language.

They were trapped by their illegal status and their inability to communicate until two of them were able to communicate with someone at Newark Airport who knew how to sign. Their plight was reported to the police, who got immigration agents, with the assistance of Spanish-speaking sign language interpreters, to raid the apartments.[1]

---

1. M. M. Cheng, "Smuggling Routes: How Mexicans Were Brought to New York," *Newsday,* 22 July 1997, 4(A); "Deaf Migrants' Families Had Feared Abuse," *Los Angeles Times,* 22 July 1997, 1(A); "For

This situation represents a worst-case scenario of the peddler-cow arrangement. While the peddlers lived in horrid conditions, the cows earned about $21,000 per week.[2] The story also points out that since opportunities for deaf Americans have improved, making them less likely to peddle, cows have had to seek out others to do their work. According to an article in *The New York Times*, "the flood of new immigrants from Latin America, Asia, and Eastern Europe in the last three decades has replenished the pool of deaf people living in isolation and need."[3]

After this incident, similar Mexican deaf peddling rings were uncovered in North Carolina, Chicago, and Los Angeles. The National Association for the Deaf (NAD) offered assistance to the peddlers, an act which brought accusations of hypocrisy from working peddlers who remembered the NAD's vehement anti-peddling campaign from the 1950s. I would like to think that NAD's new approach is evidence of progress, rather than a sign of hypocrisy. The NAD has turned its recent attention to matters of civil rights, ac-

---

Deaf Peddlers, Both Opportunity and Exploitation," *The New York Times*, 27 July 1997; R. Kim and K. Freifeld, "Smiles This Time: Mexicans Return to House Where They Were Held," *Newsday*, 23 July 1997, 5(A).

2. "For Deaf Peddlers, Both Opportunity and Exploitation," *The New York Times*, 27 July 1997.

3. Ibid.

cessibility, and communication technology—proof of a broader political focus on empowerment for the entire Deaf community.

∞

By that fall, I was slowly making my way up to Seattle. The cross-country trip didn't seem quite as glamorous as it had in the beginning; I frequently slept in my van and invented other money-saving ways to take care of my personal needs. For bathing, I would park my van in a motel parking lot early in the morning. I'd watch for motel guests to sign out, leaving the door to their rooms open. When I spotted an open room, I'd head in and take a quick shower, knowing I had some time before the maid came in to clean. It worked great and I saved a fortune. Occasionally, a maid did wander in, but I would gesture that I was deaf and hadn't heard her knock. Usually she would hustle right out, all apologies. She couldn't know I wasn't the room's official guest, just a wanderer trying to stay clean and save money.

In the beginning, many deaf peddlers find the idea of travel exciting. In the long run, however, it generally becomes mundane, boring, and stressful. To begin with, one must have a place to live. That can mean a hotel, a motel, or an apartment. When I was tired of sleeping in the van, I occasionally splurged and stayed in a low-cost motel, such as Motel 6 or Family Inn. But I got better at peddling as my trip progressed. When I started earning more money, these cheap overnight stays gave way to better digs. After a long hard day of peddling, I felt I deserved the extra comfort of a Hyatt or a Sheraton. Plus, I could afford it. And when I worked with a partner, we'd share the costs of these finer accommodations, an even better deal for both of us.

Having one's own apartment imparts a sense of stability to the restless, vagabond lifestyle of deaf peddling. But to rent an apartment, it's often necessary to prove employment. Most landlords do not consider peddling to be employment, but almost all will accept government benefits in lieu of employment.

Many landlords check credit history, which can be a problem for a deaf peddler. One way to cope with this is to deposit money in a bank account, which is then verifiable with bank statements and receipts. This is what I chose to do. Other peddlers prefer not to deal with banks, which can provide a paper trail for the Internal Revenue Service or the Social Security Administration if a question arises concerning income sources.

Another problem with renting an apartment is that landlords often require at least a six-month lease, but peddling is an unpredictable business. It's difficult to predict when one will want, or be forced, to move on. Even if a peddler could escape the attention of the authorities for long enough to rent an apartment for a few months, he or she might be forced to move on with no advance warning.

For even the most experienced deaf peddler, unpredictability defines the nature of the game. Deaf peddlers are nomads of a sort, always moving on to fresh areas. Some do manage to live in the same place for one, two, and sometimes even three years, but this takes experience and cleverness. One must study the area carefully and learn how to work it to one's advantage. Peddlers just starting out simply aren't sophisticated enough to do this, so they tend to travel all over, making mistakes, getting caught, and, in general, running themselves ragged.

∞

By December of 1986, I was exhausted from my trip. By then, I'd had enough of life on the road. I arrived in Springfield, Ohio, where my parents lived, intending to pursue my master's degree at Wright State University in Dayton. Once I'd enrolled, however, I found I needed several prerequisite courses before I could enter the program I'd chosen. So I changed my mind and started thinking about an old dream Don and I had once talked about. Back in school, we'd decided to each try for a license of some sort. His goal was to become a licensed masseur. Mine was to become a licensed pilot.

I had always wanted to fly, and now I wanted to see if my disability would stand in the way of that dream. Wright State, which was named for the Wright brothers, offered a course called "Private Pilot Ground School." Nine months later I proved to myself that it was indeed possible . . . I got my pilot's license. I called Don to chide him a bit for never having followed through on his part of the dream.

Don's situation had changed by that time. He and his girlfriend were no longer an item, and he tried to talk me into coming back to Florida and following through on our plan to peddle together. But it was too late. I had other plans, and I wasn't anxious to take that particular risk with him again. So I stayed in Ohio and looked for a real job.

I ended up getting a computer programming job at Wright Patterson Air Force Base, where my father worked, making $8 an hour—just over $300 a week before taxes. The Social Security Administration lets deaf people have up to a year in a new job before terminating their SSDI benefits, so for a while it was like having two jobs.

After a year, though, the SSDI extensions ran out. My salary was a far cry from what I could make peddling, and I felt severely underpaid. So I supplemented my income by driving into Chicago on the weekends to peddle at O'Hare International Airport. I usually earned from $750 to $1,000 a weekend during that period. I was becoming experienced at peddling, and although I didn't realize it at the time, I was moving toward a lifestyle I would never have imagined for myself.

# CHAPTER FOUR
# O'Hare and Beyond

I continued working for Wright Patterson Air Force Base, moving into a research and development project as a neural network engineer. I was working on an artificial intelligence project whose goal was to let fighter aircraft be able to fly on their own, with no pilot. My task was to increase the computer's learning speed so an aircraft could "learn" about enemy aircraft based on information in the mainframe computer on the ground.

I enjoyed the challenge of working on such a huge project. Things worked out well for the first two years, but then problems began to develop. My boss knew no sign language and didn't want to "resort" to writing in order to communicate with me. I began to feel there was no hope of advancement, which depended heavily on my relationship with my boss and on his guidance, which was minimal.

Then I met a supervisor in another department who was skilled in sign language. He used Signed English, not American Sign Language, but I assumed I would stand a much better chance for advancement with him, so I transferred to his department. Ironically, things went from bad to worse.

The philosophy he professed to have about deafness and the manner in which he actually treated me were quite different. To begin with, he was patronizing and oppressive. He would correct my signing, claiming ASL was nothing more than a form of broken English. He continually insisted I improve my signing skills and use Signed English. "Excuse me?" I wanted to say, "you, a hearing person, are correcting a deaf person who has been signing successfully all his life?"

And it was impossible to ignore the difference in the way he treated me compared to my colleagues. He spoke to me in a way he would never have spoken to them, a way that stated clearly, "You are a lesser person because of your disability."

I have never viewed myself as less of a person, less able than anyone else. A disability is nothing more than a physical inconvenience, one variation among many. Yet my new supervisor had a decided lack of respect for all deaf people. For instance, he treated his adult Sunday school students at the deaf church as if they were children, reprimanding them with a firm "Pay attention!" that smacked of paternalism.

I tried to ignore his attitude and be as professional as possible, but it was difficult. And once again, I found myself losing hope of advancement. Although there were a few other deaf people working at the air force base, they held positions as file clerks and other jobs that did not require a degree. I was the first deaf person with a college degree to work on the base, but I still felt stuck. I was beginning to understand the term *glass ceiling*.

Whenever I requested an opportunity that might help me advance, my supervisor told me I wasn't yet ready. When there was a training seminar, my boss would decide it wasn't worth the trouble to send me and that providing an interpreter would be too costly (even though it was my right and their responsibility under the Rehabilitation Act of 1973). He tried to tell me that travel was too difficult for someone who used a wheelchair and was deaf. This, despite the fact he knew I'd already managed to travel to forty-two states on my own! No matter my objections, he always found an excuse, even though the government mandated that each worker should receive forty hours of training per year. After four years I finally did get to attend a training seminar in another town—but that was only one, compared to my colleagues who attended three to four a year.

To further complicate matters, my boss received special permission to work with me on a research project. The project turned out to be research for his Ph.D. dissertation. There I was, a government employee, doing private research for my boss's personal benefit. Either he believed I wasn't competent enough to recognize the ethical problems involved in what he was asking me to do, or he had little or no respect for me.

I was furious, but had little choice if I wanted to keep my job. My boss's supervisor and he were close friends, so I had no real options. My boss even threatened that if I complained to higher levels of management that I would lose my base privileges. One of the best things about working on an air force base is the discounts you receive at the commissary. Only military personnel and base employees can shop there, and it saved me quite a bit of money. I didn't want to give up this sort of privilege, so I gave in and worked on my boss's dissertation research.

∞

As if things weren't complicated enough at my weekday job, my weekends at O'Hare developed a sudden hitch. In 1988 and 1989, passengers used baggage carriers called Smart Carts to transport their luggage through the terminal. The carts hung from a special rack, and a dollar released a cart for use. If a passenger returned her cart to a rack, she received a quarter refund. Since many passengers did not bother to return their carts for that small refund, carts were often left lying around, and homeless people who hung around the airport could collect some cash by returning them to the racks.

A homeless man in his sixties noticed that I was getting two dollars per customer, compared to his quarter per cart. He started out by merely staring at me in a menacing way, but after a while he began to accost me. I tried avoiding him, but then made the mistake of offering him a few dollars in the hope of getting him off my case. After that, of course, he began to demand money from me regularly. When I refused to keep paying him off, he retaliated by reporting me to airport employees. He knew that since he wasn't soliciting, he wasn't breaking any laws just being there.

I couldn't afford to be noticed or recognized by the O'Hare staff because being shooed away once almost guarantees that the second time there will be more than a quiet suggestion to move along. When airport employees yell loudly at peddlers, all the passengers within earshot realize that solicitation is forbidden, so they avoid further problems by not giving a peddler money. In addition to being bad for business, however, it's an extremely humiliating experience and one I was hoping to avoid.

I tried staying out of my nemesis's way as much as possible, but he roamed O'Hare from morning until night collecting those quarters. Thankfully, O'Hare officials decided to do away with the payment/refund system for the Smart Carts, perhaps because of the homeless people it attracted. After that, I never saw the man again and peddling at the airport became a lot simpler.

During this time, I heard from two old friends, Rafael and Don. Rafael and I had scarcely been in touch following our motorcycle accident four years ago. I knew he'd had a very difficult time adjusting to his injuries, though I also knew he didn't blame me for them. When we finally reconnected, he was about to graduate from the University of Puerto Rico, and we were able to talk to each other about the accident for the first time. Sometime later, I recommended Rafael for an electrical engineering job at the air force base, and we actually ended up working there together for a while.

When Don got back in touch, it turned out that he, too, had gone back to school. He was now studying to be a computer technician but was still planning on travelling and peddling, this time with another friend of his. Before he set off, we took a trip together to Greeneville, Tennessee where we visited with his aunt and uncle. Don, as changeable about his plans as ever, asked if he could come back to Ohio with me for a while. I agreed. We soon decided to buy a house together and move in as roommates.

Both of us were a bit short on cash, so my dad came up with a small business idea for us: refilling toner cartridges for businesses in our area. He invested several thousand dollars to get us started. I kept my job at the air force base while we tried to make a go of the business, but after eighteen months, Don decided there just wasn't enough money in toner cartridges. He moved to Chicago to work O'Hare International Airport as a full-time peddler, and the toner business faded away.

To help cover my expenses, I became a substitute instructor for an American Sign Language class at a local community college. The instructor had started teaching the class but then had to drop it. So several evenings a week I found myself teaching hearing college students how to sign. It was pretty ironic considering the fact that my boss at the air force base continued to complain about my sign language skills! One of the students in the class was a young woman named Sharon, who wanted to learn ASL because her mother was deaf. We got along very well with one another, and were about the same age; when the class was over, we began to see one another socially.

∞

I wasn't ready to quit my job, even though I was unhappy, but I was still travelling to O'Hare on weekends to supplement my income. The Dayton Airport was actually much closer, but the money was too good to pass up at O'Hare. Anyplace I could make $1,000 a weekend was well worth the commute. Plus, there was something else I had to consider. My parents were ashamed of my peddling and asked me not to peddle within a fifty-mile radius of their home. They were afraid I'd run into people they knew, and I respected their wishes.

At this point I had a lot in common with the other deaf peddlers I met. Having realized that the traveling life isn't as exciting as I thought it was, I now peddled for one reason, to pay my bills. Most peddlers are out there doing exactly the same thing. Rarely will you find someone peddling for extra spending money or for money to put away in savings. And of course some peddlers are trying to support addictions: marijuana, cocaine, alcohol. But for whatever reason it's used, the primary motivation for peddling is income.

Still, a peddler always needs to consider how hard he'll have to work and how great his actual earnings will be per hour. Earnings vary greatly according to each peddler's attitude and motivation. I found that

*Figure 2*

one way to increase my profits was to be more creative in the wares that I offered. I had been using the traditional pamphlet that Don had first showed me when we roomed together at Gallaudet. But after a while, the costs of printing became too high. Plus, the printers complained about the cutting, folding, collating, and stapling involved. So I decided to come up with a new design. Hiring a graphic designer to come up with a new pamphlet would have been expensive. But, luckily, my sister is an artist and I was able to tell her what I wanted.

My new flyer (shown in figure 2) consisted of one piece with only one fold, as opposed to the multi-page stapled pamphlet. Only the manual alphabet and sixteen basic signs were shown inside, with a few learning suggestions on the back. The printer was thrilled at its ease of production. It only cost one or two cents to print, despite the fact I ordered two colors of ink.

∞

Don and I started yet another business on the side, a multilevel marketing business, but it wasn't bringing in much money. We sold Melacula, an Australian oil used for personal hygiene and external medical care. We distributed it to people and then convinced them to join the "family tree." They would then make money from people down the line who sold the product. We earned a percentage of their commissions. To attract people into the business, we set up special meetings twice a week or attended deaf events where we could pass out flyers and tell people about our business. The business didn't bring in enough money alone to support us, perhaps $500 to $1,000 a month, but it supplemented our other earnings.

Don was constantly trying to persuade me to quit my job and join him as a full-time peddler at O'Hare, but I still hoped that things would turn around for me at Wright Patterson. Well, things did change—but unfortunately not for the better.

I had been working at Wright Patterson for about five years by then. Usually when I called in sick I used the voice relay service, but for some reason that morning it was terribly busy and I couldn't get through. I ended up leaving my boss three voice messages just to make sure he would understand my message clearly.

When I returned to work the following day, he informed me he'd been unable to understand my messages and accused me of abusing my sick time and personal leave privileges. Then he announced he was putting it on my record.

It was too much. I gave two weeks' notice. Unluckily for him, his dissertation research wasn't yet complete, and he was furious. He complained that the government had wasted money by paying my interpreting expenses for a week-long training session in West Virginia—news to me, especially since I'd never had the opportunity to go out of state for any training. I pointed out to him that a good supervisor would have tried to work out the differences between us. But it was too late for that. I felt I'd tried my best. Now it was time to try something new.

I had no intention of making peddling my life. The multilevel marketing business still wasn't bringing in very much money, so I decided to start my own small business. I bought an Orbotron, one of those spherical steel devices you see at fairs and carnivals. A person is strapped in and then gets the ride of his or her life, rotating in all different directions. At the time, I thought this would be an interesting way to make a living, but the hassles of permits, licenses, and the huge amount of liability insurance required made the venture impossible to continue. All it left me with was debt, so I returned to peddling. This time, however, I decided to try peddling as a full-time job.

Sharon and I were now dating, even though she had been shocked to learn about my peddling. Her mother had always had a job despite being deaf, and told her children that peddling was wrong. I explained that I was doing it to make money, and told her how much money I could make in a very short time. I told her that I hated working with people who were condescending towards deaf people, or with people who didn't know sign language. Although she never totally agreed with my need to peddle, Sharon slowly accepted the fact that it was what I wanted to do.

So I rented out the house Don and I owned, and moved to Chicago with Sharon. We rented a two-bedroom apartment and Don moved in with us.

At that time there were only a few regular peddlers at O'Hare: Joan, who was seventy and had been a peddler for many years; Ted and Lynn, a husband and wife team; Don; and now myself. O'Hare was the world's busiest airport, serving sixty-four million customers every year. Because of its central U.S. location, O'Hare is a hub, a point of connection for people flying all over the world. In other words, O'Hare was a peddler's dream.

We peddlers found that O'Hare was a great place to avoid burnout. Burnout doesn't refer to the peddler, but to the customer base. Staying in one place guarantees that you will start to run into customers you've already approached. Customers may buy once, but rarely twice. In small towns, this can happen after only a day or two. So even if a peddler is not noticed and not asked to move on, saturation of the customer base will eventually occur and it will become necessary to look for new places to peddle.

Peddlers at O'Hare, however, enjoyed a constantly changing customer base, lax security, and more than enough business for five peddlers. Plus, the five of us got along well, easily agreeing to work different concourses, chatting when we ran into one another. Things were so good that Don talked his brother and sister-in-law, Nelly (both of whom were deaf), into moving to Chicago. His brother wanted nothing to do with peddling, but Nelly brought our group to six.

The number continued to increase and soon we were ten: two new arrivals, plus Ted's sister-in-law, Barb, who had moved to Chicago with Ted's brother and their four children. Barb was supporting the family by peddling. Last, but not least, there was Mike, the newest member of the ranks. Mike had peddled on and off in the Chicago area for years. He had a scruffy appearance and a rough air about him, and peddled to support a drug addiction. The ten of us worked as a team and often had lunch together.

The brochures used by a peddler or a group of peddlers is their trademark. Selling the same novelty and using the same brochure allows a group to mark its territory. I showed the group the mini-tool keychain I had started using in Los Angeles. We liked the idea of selling a product along with a pamphlet, but the sets I had bought from California rusted and fell apart easily. I paid only $390 per case, but they looked cheap and I was embarrassed to sell them.

The keychains were made in Hong Kong, and a friend of mine frequently flew there on business. He loved to go into the city's marketplaces, and I asked him to keep his eye out for a similar set that was better made.

My friend soon returned from Hong Kong with a good deal. A case of 2,400 keychains would cost $485, but the product was clearly of far better quality. In addition, I was able to arrange for the workers at the factory to assemble the kits. Until then, I had been stuffing the keychain and the case flap into each case, thousands and thousands of them. With this new product, all I had to do was staple them to the cards. The convenience cost me $50 more per case, but it was well worth it. We decided to place a large wholesale order to get the best possible price. Our peddling group agreed to sell the keychains for $2.50, but soon reduced the price to $2 because making change was a hassle. With this new trinket, we were able to maximize our earning potential.

It seemed like a good time to change the brochure as well. The one my sister had designed provided a complete explanation up front, and I adapted it so it read more like a booklet. The cover of the new pamphlet (shown in figure 3) caught the customer's attention, and then the inside featured some useful basic signs, as well as an explanation of the keychain and why I was selling it. A poem about the spirit of spring appeared on the back of the booklet.

Figure 3

During this time, Don met a new girlfriend. Jan, who was also deaf, worked in a downtown Chicago bank for minimum wage. He'd visit her in her low-income, government-subsidized apartment and spread out his cash on the bed. Jan was astonished and it wasn't long before there was one more peddler at O'Hare.

We weren't the only ones at the airport taking advantage of the lax security and safe, indoor environment. Places like O'Hare, which are huge and open twenty-four hours a day, are popular spots for homeless people. One day as I was heading down the corridor on a concourse, I saw a man picking through the trash. I stopped and watched him for a while, wondering what he would do when he found something. He pulled a half-empty beer cup out of the trash, picked out a cigarette butt, and drank the beer! Then he searched again and came up with some grapes. By that time, he knew he had an audience and proceeded to make a show of it, pulling the grapes off one by one and popping each into his mouth. Perhaps he saw the rest of the population as fools who threw away perfectly good food, while he took full advantage of it. In spite of the situation, his antics made me laugh. I was making a good living at that time. I had food on my table and a roof over my head, and it was eye-opening to encounter people who had absolutely nothing.

※

For a while, Don, Jan, Sharon, and I all lived together. But soon we began to argue. Our views differed, and we wondered if there were too many of us living in too small a space. But even a larger apartment didn't help, and Sharon and I decided it was time to tell Don and Jan to move out on their own.

Aside from the awkwardness at home, things were going along well at O'Hare. Occasionally, they went very well. One afternoon in United Concourse C, I approached a gate area filled with people waiting for a boarding announcement. I passed out my wares as usual, and then came back to collect money. One customer, a chubby lady in her seventies, was still reading my card. She had rosy cheeks, a beehive hairdo, and seemed like the kind, grandmotherly type. She looked me over, as if she were trying to decide if I had a real disability or not, and then shoved her hand inside her purse and took out a small, old-fashioned wallet. I glanced away, not wanting to stare while she pulled out her money, and didn't realize until I looked down at the bill that it was a hundred. I clasped her hand warmly to show my appreciation, and she pinched my cheek as if I were a little boy. Usually, that would have bothered me, but this time I didn't mind at all.

I discovered that some members of our team set their earning goals at $500 or even $1,000 dollars a day during a peak season such as Christmas. Occasionally we met peddlers from outside the Chicago area who were coming into the city to peddle, and often one would mention earning only $100 over a period of several hours. We veterans would nod and say something like, "Wow, that's good!" when, in truth, we knew it wasn't good at all. But we weren't anxious to share our secrets. We tended to discourage out-of-towners, telling them there were already many peddlers around, that the police were strict, and the money wasn't very good. More often than not, they believed us and moved on. Looking back on it, it seems we'd come to feel that Chicago was our territory, and we wished to remain the city's kings and queens.

Yet the Charles Dickens' line, "It was the best of times, it was the worst of times," could easily apply to my time at O'Hare. The worst of times were still to come.

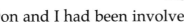

Don and I had been involved in several business ventures together over the years: our movie fests at Gallaudet, the ill-fated toner cartridges, the multilevel marketing business, and now the peddling. By January 1994, we'd been partners in the marketing business for several years when I decided it wasn't something I wanted to continue doing. I decided to withdraw my involvement in the business.

Don was not only disappointed in my decision, he was furious. I simply decided to back off, assuming he'd get over it in time, and we continued seeing each other around O'Hare. In retrospect, though, it's clear to me that this was the beginning of the deterioration of our relationship.

I started getting fed up with working as a group, and the problems with Don didn't help matters any. I decided to work as an independent and started buying my own brochures and novelties. Working by myself, I found that $2.50 was a good price for the keychain because people often gave me $3 and told me to keep the change. The other peddlers began to view me more as a competitor than an ally. About the time I split from the group, they ran out of brochures and asked me to provide them with another design to take to the printer. I told them, "Sorry, but you're on your own now." They ended up having to pool their resources to pay a professional designer $300 to develop a new brochure.

Working as a unit, it had been our habit to agree to split one concourse in half. We'd work our way out from the center every forty-five minutes or so, timing the pattern with flight arrivals. There was great money to be made that way. But with no spirit of teamwork left, things deteriorated and peddlers fought to grab the best areas. We even began to adjust the prices of the keychains, just so we could compete against one another.

To show their hostility for my lack of cooperation and my new-found independence, the other peddlers began to try to interfere with my peddling. They would watch for me and then congregate at the very gates I was heading for, beating me to the territory. Or one of the peddlers might point me out to the security police.

At first, I tried not to let their animosity bother me. But gradually it started to wear me down. There are six main concourses at O'Hare, and there were now eleven deaf peddlers. And ten of them were doing their best to put me out of business.

Normally, we could have worked each concourse in

pairs, but they would arrive before me and divide up the turf so I wouldn't have a chance to sell. Still, I managed to make good money through sheer stubborn persistence. You have to understand that I was a different person when I worked O'Hare . . . absolutely focused on working fast and maximizing my earnings. I was aggressive and successful, a real threat to their livelihood. While they were involved in an arrangement that required them to share their earnings, I kept everything I made for myself. As long as I worked there, I lowered their collective earning potential.

It occurred to me that if the other peddlers didn't see evidence of my presence (that is, if they didn't see my unique brochure around the airport), I wouldn't have to worry so much about their interference. So I copied their new brochure on my computer and began to use it. When they discovered what I had done, they were furious. But by then, we were all playing the same mean-spirited game, all of us caught up in the business of selling a bit of our souls with each new transaction. And without the spirit of cooperation that had helped us all, there was very little left but plain and simple greed.

Before long, Don and his group tried to force me out by buying our supplier's entire inventory of mini-tool keychains. Don refused to sell any to me and also forbade any of the other peddlers to do so. But I'd been working O'Hare for ten years by then, and I knew ways to work around just about anything. I found a different supplier and was right back in business. They'd ended up investing a lot of money for nothing, and our nasty game escalated even further.

To get to Concourse C in the United terminal, one has to pass through a long tunnel. The tunnel has steep escalators at each end. Although I use a wheelchair, I have a lot of experience with escalators and have become pretty skilled at holding on tightly to the moving handrail with both hands. I hate to use elevators because they waste valuable time, and when you're a peddler, time is money.

One day I was riding the escalator when Don saw me coming. He pushed the emergency stop button when I was about halfway to the top. There I was, stuck at the middle of that long, steep escalator with Don above me, laughing. I was forced to bump my chair backwards, down one step at a time, until I was at the bottom again. I headed straight for the elevator, telling myself to think positively and not let what had just happened bother me. But when I finally got to the concourse, Don and some of the other peddlers had already staked their claim.

Mike, the last peddler to join the group, had always aroused my concern. His drug addiction made him seem desperate, capable of just about anything. He started harassing me in small ways. First, he dumped a glass of water into my backpack, which I kept on the back of my wheelchair and used to carry my wares. He was hoping to ruin everything I planned to sell that day, and if I hadn't normally kept things in plastic bags, he would have succeeded.

The very next time I used the escalator Mike used Don's trick of pressing the stop button. He did it again and again over the next several days, always when I was halfway up or halfway down. Finally, I had to start using the elevator.

I was boiling with anger. Of course, my customers had no idea what I was feeling inside, no idea what was going on around them among the deaf peddlers. Yet instead of wearing me down, their harassment actually ended up having the opposite effect. If their goal was to get me out of O'Hare, then I would never leave. I vowed to keep going no matter what. And, in fact, I became determined to find their weakness and exploit it.

One thing I did have in my favor was the attitude of the O'Hare security police. Even when the other peddlers reported my presence, or were themselves arrested, the police never arrested me. They'd simply gesture and say "Get out!" They didn't seem to want to be bothered arresting a disabled peddler if it meant they'd have to find a way to get him and his wheelchair to the police station.

There were, however, a few younger detectives who worked undercover at the airport. It was their job to keep an eye out for people stealing luggage and so forth. And there were other illegal activities going on at the airport. For instance, I ran across a man one day who offered to sell me a $600 dollar necklace (or so he said) for $50, before he realized I had my own wares to peddle. I saw him many times after that, but we kept our distance. Then one day he was arrested by one of the undercover detectives. That same detective had never given me much of a problem. If he saw me working, he'd simply flash his police badge and gesture at me to move along, which I did. But, of course, I always came back.

∞

One morning I arrived at the airport at a very early hour, trying to make sure I wouldn't be out-turfed by Don's team. When they arrived later in the morning, they seemed particularly frustrated to find me already there and working.

When I finally decided to move on to another concourse, I saw Don ahead of me, going in the same direction. I hurried to pass him, which, it turned out, was a big mistake. I came abreast of him in an isolated area, and suddenly he whirled around and punched me in the face. Don, who used to be my best friend, was attacking me! I wasn't able to fight back, but I was so boiling mad that I took off after him, following him straight into an area reserved for business-class passengers. The area offered free beverages, and Don served himself a glass of orange juice and then dashed it in my face.

I sat there, angry and humiliated. But even then, my stubbornness won out. It simply wasn't in my nature to give up and go home, so I cleaned myself up as best I could and worked hard all that day, sticky orange juice and all.

Looking back, we peddlers shouldn't have worked so hard to make things difficult for one another; things were going to get tough enough without the added complication of in-fighting. Perhaps because there were too many peddlers and the detectives were tired of seeing us day after day, the airport finally decided to crack down. No longer were we simply told to move along. Now the security police told us to move along and followed until we actually left the premises. I decided the pressure was too much to bear. A week or so after the airport stopped tolerating its peddlers, I moved to Midway Airport on the southwest side of Chicago, where the money was good and the problems were fewer.

I didn't completely stop peddling at O'Hare, and when I returned there on occasion the security was increasingly tighter. Probably a great deal of it had to do with the 1993 World Trade Center bombing, after which the Federal Aviation Administration declared all airports were high-security areas. The number of detectives at O'Hare suddenly skyrocketed. Don was the first peddler to be arrested, but he wouldn't be the last.

∞

Don was put in jail and released after a few hours, with a requirement to show up in court at a later date. Luckily for him, he'd already made plans to move to Atlanta with Jan, who was now his wife. So, with his promise to leave the Chicago area, his lawyer was able to get him off.

Before he left Chicago, I called Don and asked if we could bury the hatchet. We had been friends for a long time, and it seemed a shame to let anger and stubbornness ruin that. Besides, I was just plain tired of competing with him, and, it turned out, he was just as tired of competing with me. It had been quite a showdown, and we'd both proven our mettle. But now it was time to put it all behind us. He readily agreed; it seemed that neither of us had realized we'd lost two whole years of friendship because of our ridiculous peddler war.

Just before he left for Atlanta, Don gave me all the keychains he had left. He informed the other peddlers they'd have to contact me if they wanted more. It was something of a joke, considering everything that had been going on. "What? Buy from Dennis?" they said. They didn't know what to think. But they had little choice, and my Hong Kong friend still has several deaf peddlers in the Chicago area buying their keychain sets through him.

The ranks were thinning, but still I stayed. Even though I knew my days of deaf peddling at O'Hare were numbered, I ended up pushing my luck a little too far.

I kept going back. I tried to be discreet, but one detective—the same one who used to let me off with nothing more than a warning—had had enough. He came up to me one day, stressing his words with emphatic gestures. "You," he said, "out! One more time, jail, jail!"

For some reason, I didn't take his warning seriously. I signed and mouthed, "Okay, okay, I'm going home now," but all I did was proceed to another concourse and start selling again. There, two detectives came running up to me, and this time it was the real thing—"true business," as we say in ASL.

They escorted me outside the airport and over to a big police van with bars on the windows. I was actually going to jail! And, I thought, I probably deserved it. I'd been peddling for many years, despite repeated warnings, never taking even one of them seriously. Now it was time to pay the piper. Except for one thing: the van wasn't wheelchair accessible.

When the detectives realized this, it was back inside the airport and up to their office, where they ticketed me and explained that from now on there would be many more police officers, greater pressure on the peddlers, and tickets every time someone was seen peddling. Not to mention the very real possibility of jail . . . that is, if they could transport me there.

Things didn't go quite as well for the airport's other remaining peddlers. The end of deaf peddling at O'Hare couldn't have come at a worse time for Ted and Lynn. They were in serious financial trouble, with $40,000 worth of credit card debt. A few years before, we'd talked about how easy it was to get credit cards, even without a job. With thirty cards in my name, I was living proof. Of course, I'd realized pretty quickly how unwise it was to have access to all that credit, and I'd cut most of mine up. But Ted and Lynn decided to see if they could top my thirty. They almost did. They managed to get twenty-eight cards, all with high interest rates. And then they used them! They were paying $1,500 dollars a month just in credit card payments, plus the living expenses for two adults and four children.

Lynn was fully aware of how dangerous it had become to peddle at O'Hare, but she felt she had no choice. She had to pay their bills. And, of course, she was arrested. She cried and pantomimed to the detective that she had four children and how would they eat, etc., etc. Luckily for her, it worked. The detective let her go with only a stern warning.

Would you believe she actually had the nerve to go back again? She, Mike, and Nelly were all peddling together when a detective grabbed Lynn by the arm and told Mike and Nelly to follow him. Mike and Nelly panicked and took off running. Now, Mike and Nelly were both in terrible shape. Somehow, though, they managed to outrun the police. Perhaps their fear of arrest produced an adrenaline rush that gave them superhuman power! They ran down the stairs, turning this way and that, trying to run in a maze pattern so they would lose the cops, managed to make it to the parking lot, jumped into their car, and took off. They told me later that after driving for a while they suddenly had to pull over. With all the stress and exertion, they both ended up losing their breakfasts on the side of the road. But they didn't get caught!

Unfortunately, Lynn wasn't so lucky. She ended up with a ticket and a court date, and to make matters worse, her husband Ted was arrested that very same day. At last they finally got the idea and started making plans to move to Texas.

I had my own problems, though. Because I had been ticketed, I had to appear in court. Of course I knew I was guilty, but I wanted to avoid having peddling on my record. The prosecutor wasn't particularly pleased when she learned I would plead not guilty, and before the trial she told me that if I was found guilty I would be fined $50 plus court costs, and if I pleaded not guilty I would be fined $500. I told her I still planned to plead not guilty. "You're costing the state money," she said, "therefore, we refuse to provide you with a public defender."

Now this seemed strange. I'm not an expert on the law, but I was under the impression that a person has the right to be supplied with a public defender if he doesn't have his own lawyer.

Lynn was supposed to have appeared in court that day as well, but never showed up. The judge announced he was putting out an arrest warrant for her with a $200 fine. This didn't make sense. Lynn, who had failed to appear, was being fined less than I, who had shown up. The prosecutor's threat was clearly coercion to get me to plead guilty.

Instead of entering my plea of not guilty, the prosecutor informed the judge that I had requested a lawyer of my own choosing. The judge delayed the trial two months, and I hired a lawyer. When we went back to court, the judge agreed to drop the case if I promised not to go back to O'Hare again, at least for the purpose of peddling. I agreed. I was finally finished at O'Hare, but I wasn't finished with peddling.

# CHAPTER FIVE

# On My Own

I decided to move to Florida for the fresh air and sunshine, and settled in Orlando because of the huge number of tourists passing through the city's airport. After Chicago, Orlando felt like paradise.

Orlando International Airport is much smaller than O'Hare, yet my earnings in Florida were higher. I called it the *paradise influence*. Florida is vacation land; most people passing through the Orlando airport are on their way to have fun. They are heading to Disney World, EPCOT Center, or some other pleasant attraction. Their moods are high, they are excited to be in Orlando, and they are more than willing to give a couple of dollars to a deaf peddler. I would say that as much as 70 percent of those I approached bought something from me, compared to only 30 percent at O'Hare. This extremely high rate brought in very good earnings.

But after a while, I began to sense that things were not perfect. It seemed that the airport staff was noticing my presence. The airport installed two surveillance cameras, and I noticed that at least one camera always seemed to be deliberately looking for me. As much as I

tried to avoid its range, it was as if the camera's operator was following my every move.

One day when this was happening, I decided to
leave the airport. On my way out, I kept an eye on the
cameras stationed on my exit route. True to my suspi-
cions, these cameras, too, seemed to be following my
movements. I would scoot out of range, feeling like I
was sneaking away from a giant eyeball, and then when
I disappeared from its view it would wiggle as though
the operator was straining to pick me up again. It was
actually quite funny.

After that, it was easy to know when a camera found
me. Instead of its usual slow arcing motion, it would
suddenly become focused on me. Lights! Camera! Ac-
tion! There was no question I was being watched, and I
spent a lot of time dodging in and out of range. I got a
kick out of evading the "eye" by staying straight be-
neath the camera, at an angle it simply couldn't achieve.

One day, an airport security person came up to me.
He seemed perturbed. I acted nonchalant and signaled
to him that I was deaf. He motioned for me to follow
him toward the exit, which I did, and indicated that he
was waiting for the police to come. "Police?" I ques-
tioned, and asked him to write things down for me so
we could communicate clearly. At first, he seemed to
think I was joking, but I indicated I was serious about
wanting a paper and pencil.

He wrote me a note. "We're waiting for the police
to come."

"Sure," I wrote back. Then, "I'd like to request an interpreter."

"Writing will be just fine," he answered. Then he asked, "Can you read my lips?"

It was an infuriating question. "Can you read my signs?" I signed.

When a police officer finally arrived, the two of them engaged in a spoken conversation, presumably about me, and none of it was written down for me.

Finally, they wrote me a note. "What's your name? Do you have any ID?"

I did not have any identification on me that day and mouthed the words, "at home." I had learned from experience *never* to carry identification because without it I often got off with a verbal warning. Police officers seemed less apt to want the hassle of arresting someone with no ID, especially someone who hadn't committed a felony.

This police officer was more insistent, however. He asked me to write down my name, then my birth date and Social Security number.

"You're not allowed to peddle around here," he wrote.

I wrote back, "This airport employee has violated my rights by refusing to provide an interpreter for this conversation." I explained that under the Americans with Disabilities Act, it was my right to have an interpreter—especially since a police officer was involved and the situation was fast becoming a legal matter. I insisted they provide me with the interpreter required under the law. "I know my rights," I wrote. I also knew that if they were violated, it would be likely that a court would dismiss my case.

I knew perfectly well at this point that I was going out of my way to give them a hard time. Still, I also knew that my demand was legally accurate.

They stared at me.

"Do you know what a TDD is?" the officer wrote.

Of course I knew what a TDD was. I indicated my puzzlement that he would ask such a question. I guess I must have passed his test and proved I really was deaf because he wrote, "Okay, never mind," and then added, "I'm giving you a verbal warning this time, but the next time I see you here peddling, you will be arrested."

"Okay, I'm sorry," I said, and the officer escorted me away.

But I was too used to verbal warnings to stay away long. A month later I was back at the airport, and within minutes I was caught. This time it was a different security person and a different police officer. But they both knew I had already been caught there once and they called for an interpreter without my asking. When she arrived about forty-five minutes later, she turned out to be a very nervous fingerspeller. Her hands shook with every letter, and the communication was slow and torturous.

Finally, the officer grew impatient. He prepared a

long written document, which we both ended up signing in several places. It stated that I understood and acknowledged why I was in trouble. It had been a relatively short stay in Orlando.

∞

I decided to start traveling from city to city. Yet I found
I was running out of options—I had been caught in Orlando, Chicago, and some of the country's other major
airports. Even though I had the experience to make
even more money then ever, I started to realize I was
dissatisfied with the peddler lifestyle. Even as I was
selling keychains to strangers, I began to think about
going back to school for my master's degree.

After Orlando, I headed to Atlanta's Hatsfield Airport. It was a relatively easy place to peddle. The police
were veteran cops, but there weren't enough of them,
and as a result they didn't check all the concourses regularly. If they did happen to see me, they did little more
than shake a finger and say, "Uh-uh-uh, don't do that."

Yet, on the other hand, there can be differences in security even within an airport. When I first started peddling there, I headed for Delta. Delta used three of Hatsfield's six concourses, and I assumed the busiest gates
would bring in the most business. Yet I noticed immediately that the Delta staff seemed to be more watchful for
peddlers and for others hanging around. There was a
crispness in their manner and an overall strictness at
the Delta gates that was missing in other areas of the airport, and often the Delta staff would come up and shoo
us away. Of course I understood that was their job, and

had to grudgingly commend them for doing it well. As a result, I was careful not to go to the Delta gates every day.

In addition to security, there are a lot of differences between the people at different gates within an airport. My experience at Hatsfield taught me how socioeconomic factors could influence the peddling business, sometimes in unexpected ways. Peddlers are always talking about *location,* a term which refers to specific concourses and gates when used in reference to an airport. It also includes specific airlines. Of course, deaf peddlers prefer working the concourses of major airlines simply due to the larger volume of passenger traffic. Whereas the gates of a minor airline might only have passenger traffic every two hours or so, a peddler can work a major airline's gates all day long with no let-up.

Yet even when Delta's security was being lenient, I still found myself having to hustle to make my usual amounts. I can't say for certain why this was so, but I do have a theory. The Delta concourses catered to business passengers who paid big ticket prices because either they or their companies could afford to. They seemed reluctant to shell out even a few more dollars to a peddler. They haughtily brushed us off, even though they appeared to have money. There were a few gates at Delta where I occasionally earned nothing at all, which was very rare; and it wasn't unusual to work all forty-plus gates on the concourse and earn less than $100, sometimes as little as $30.

ValuJet had only half as many gates as Delta, but it turned out to be a great place to peddle. The ValuJet market consisted of travelers who couldn't afford the major airline fares. ValuJet was a fairly new airline, a small company that did good business by offering cheap fairs. The passengers didn't have an attitude toward me, they were "just folks." Although (and maybe because) they were traveling cheaply, they were still willing to spend a few dollars for a peddler's wares. I found that if I worked the ValuJet concourse diligently, I could earn $700 a day with rarely a threat of getting in trouble.

After the ValuJet crash in the Everglades in May of 1996, however, things changed drastically. The airline closed for several months and when it did resume flights, it only resumed a small percentage of them. As a result, it was no longer worthwhile to peddle on their concourse.

∞

Aside from class distinctions, cultural differences also affect a peddler's choice of location. When I first decided to peddle international concourses—where flights were arriving from and departing for countries such as Belgium, Germany, Holland, India, Japan, Mexico, and England—I had no idea what to expect. I soon learned that international gates are a much different story from gates for domestic flights.

I experimented first at the British Airways gates, where most flights were leaving for London. The first gate I approached was full of people. I passed out my merchandise and then went back to retrieve it or collect money. I earned $100 at that one gate, an unbelievably good amount!

After that experience, I was thrilled to notice another London flight scheduled at a nearby gate, which meant less time lost wheeling around from concourse to concourse. I could concentrate my effort on these international gates and earn more money more easily. I discovered quickly that the British were the most lucrative international gates and that, more specifically, flights departing for London or Gatwick were the most productive. The British customers were friendly and generous, often giving $10 with no expectation of getting change.

With my good experience at the London gates, I moved on to other European destinations hoping for the same response. I was disappointed, however. Gates serving Brussels and Germany produced so-so earnings, with Paris about the same or maybe a little worse. These passengers weren't as open to the idea of interacting with a peddler and I found my earnings to be only about $10 per gate.

Many peddlers avoid international gates because the customers tend to give them coins instead of bills. Apparently passengers leaving the country are anxious to get rid of change. I didn't mind so much, as long as I was making the sales—but there were times when my shirt pockets were so full of change, I was constantly shoveling it into my backpack!

After Hatsfield, I went to Canada, then on to Los Angeles, San Francisco, and Salt Lake City. I jumped around often to be sure I didn't wear out my welcome in any one airport. Two weeks was the longest I could stay without being kicked out by airport security.

I gradually learned that inexperience can be expensive, both in terms of money and energy. I began to slow down and use my head. I started plotting destinations on a map, circling areas I had worked in or planned to go to next. I established a pattern. In the winter months, I worked in the southern states, enjoying the warm weather. I'd head north for the summer months, working my way easterly back across the northern states, where it was cooler, gradually making a big circle.

In addition to weather, I also began to take into account the individual airports I targeted. As I had learned in Orlando and Chicago, the character of each airport depends greatly on the police that patrol it. In the St. Louis Lambert Airport, for example, a police officer came up to me once and shook his finger. Then he noticed my keychains. "Gee," he said, "I could use some small screwdrivers like that." It was an ironic moment, especially considering why I had left Orlando and Chicago.

I also began to study the different methods I had seen peddlers use. There are as many different techniques as there are peddlers, and just as many types of pamphlets. Some peddlers put a lot of time and energy into their pamphlets; others may use ripped and smudged photocopies of a pamphlet they found thirty

*Figure 4*

years ago. As I met different deaf peddlers around the country, it became my habit to keep copies of their pamphlets. I enjoyed collecting them, sampling the different designs they used. Plus, each one reminds me of the person who sold it.

Figure 4 shows a small card I got from an older deaf peddler who had minimal language skills, even in ASL. He worked under a cow and was very loyal to him. Although he wasn't very educated, he'd learned a great deal from his travels and was a hard worker, showing up at O'Hare at five-thirty in the morning and working until nine every night. The front of his card gives his sales pitch, while the back shows the manual alphabet. I talked with him a bit and he said his card made him good money, despite the fact it didn't look like a good seller. It was definitely cheap to print because it is small and uses only one ink color. He probably paid a cent for every two or three cards. I met another deaf man who peddled internationally. He'd been to many countries—Germany, France, Switzerland, Italy. He used pamphlets with different languages, depending on the country he was peddling in! He was about forty years old, and had been a peddler for about half his life. A fascinating gentleman, he was very adept at communicating through a combination of mimes and gestures. He, too, worked from five-thirty to eight, staying a few weeks in different U.S. cities and motivating himself with a trip abroad every six months or so. He and a partner worked under a boss who took care of his men's needs and chose the sites where they worked.

His pamphlet, titled *American Sign Language*, is shown in figure 5. The inside of the pamphlet shows the manual alphabet and several basic signs. This is a nice basic design, cheap to print because it only uses colored paper and black ink. Generally, a plain paper flyer such as this doesn't have great earning potential, but he seemed well pleased with it.

The design shown in figure 6 is what I call the low-budget special. I don't even remember who gave me this card, which is Spartan, even chintzy. It's just a small

*Figure 5*

card with a solicitation message on the front and some hard-to-read pictures of the manual alphabet on the back. I can't imagine that the peddlers who use this card make much money. It's neither interesting nor impressive. Note the reference to the peddler as a deaf-mute, an old-fashioned term. I would guess this card originated in the 1970s, and is probably still in use today. I always believed in keeping up-to-date and trying to offer potential customers an interesting product.

The design shown in figure 7 is an improvement, although it too is a simple, two-sided card. The language on the front, which refers to the seller's "college expenses," usually helps a sale. Customers like to feel

**SMILE**

DEAF –
EDUCATION –
– SYSTEM

Please pardon my intrusion, but I
am a DEAF-MUTE trying to earn a
living. I have a family to support.
  Would you help me by buying one
of these cards.

Pay   whatever   you
wish....

THANK   YOU   AND
MAY   GOD   BLESS
YOU   ALL.

OVER

*Figure 6*

SMILE
HAVE A NICE

DAY

**Ladies and Gentlemen**

*I am a deaf-person selling
these Sign Language
Cards to make my living
through College expenses.*

**Will you kindly buy one?**

*Pay Any Price You Wish
Thank You for Your
Kindness.*

(over)

*Figure 7*

they are helping someone toward a goal, even though
they have no way of knowing if the peddler is a college
student or not. Back in the 1970s, when this card was
probably developed, deaf people were just beginning
to claim the civil rights guaranteed them under the Rehabilitation Act of 1973, which stated that publicly
funded educational institutions (among other entities)
must be accessible to all students. Although deaf students had been attending Gallaudet College in Washington, D.C., and the National Technical Institute for
the Deaf in Rochester, New York, for several years, the

idea of a deaf person attending college was still something of a novelty, especially in the eyes of hearing customers. By the 1980s, it had become less unusual.

When a pamphlet states vaguely that its sale is helping the peddler make a living, it can mean almost anything, including that the money will go toward the support of a drug or alcohol problem or toward the purchase of luxuries. A reference to education, like the first pamphlet Don showed me, is another story. I often let people know that I was a college student. However, their questions about which school I was attending got too time-consuming and cumbersome. I later changed the wording on my pamphlets to read "living and educational expenses."

The design shown in figure 8 adds an interesting twist, featuring a picture of Popeye on the cover. It opens to show basic signs, the manual alphabet, and some hand shadow pictures. The back panel shows the Lord's Prayer. The peddler who used this design had stayed with it for some time and felt no need to change. I worked with him from time to time and whenever I brought up the subject of switching to a different design, he'd protest, saying it was too expensive and that he'd rather stick with the tried and true.

The peddler who used the Popeye pamphlet was a bright man, but not particularly motivated. He came from an all-deaf family and attended Gallaudet for a while before withdrawing. Apparently he didn't care for the academic life with its homework, projects, and

### American Manual Alphabet

Hand alphabet used by the Deaf
throughout the world. Easy to learn.

**MAKE FUN OF SHADOW PICTURES**
Be the life of the party,
show it to your friends, etc.

### THE LORD'S PRAYER

OUR FATHER, who art in heaven,
Hallowed by thy name. Thy Kingdom
come. THY WILL BE DONE, on
earth, as it is in heaven. Give us this
day our daily bread. And forgive us
our trespasses as we forgive those who
trespass against us. And lead us not
into temptation, but deliver us from
evil: FOR THINE IS THE
KINGDOM AND THE POWER,
AND THE GLORY, FOREVER.

AMEN

I LOVE
YOU

**DEAF -**

**EDUCATIONAL**

**- SYSTEM**

*Ladies and Gentlemen*

I AM A **DEAF** PERSON SELLING
THESE MINI-BOOKLETS TO IM-
PROVE OUR COMMUNICATION.

**DONATION    —    $1.00**
**WILL BE DEEPLY APPRECIATED**

THANK YOU
FOR YOUR KINDNESS

*Figure 8*

deadlines; he wanted to work where and when he pleased. He would go to O'Hare for only a few hours, just long enough to meet his daily expenses.

His pamphlet was actually a fairly inexpensive printing job, just black ink on eye-catching hot pink paper. Although bright colors do attract people's attention, I avoided them for that exact reason. A peddler wants to avoid attracting the attention of the wrong people, namely airport personnel or police. I preferred beige, which presented an attractive pamphlet that wouldn't attract too much attention.

At one point I did experiment with color. I'd grown tired of using the same old flyer and began using three variations of the same flyer. One was printed on yellow cardstock, which symbolized the rising sun, and led off with "Good Morning." The second was green for the color of grass and said "Good Afternoon." The third was dark blue, for the evening sky, and said "Good Evening." I had to keep my eye on the time and use the right pamphlet to match the time of day. This marketing gimmick was good for sales, but I soon tired of changing the pamphlet three times a day and dropped the idea.

Changing the pamphlets on a seasonal basis was a lot simpler. I had several different designs with seasonal themes, such as the Fourth of July. (Inside the pamphlet were the manual alphabet, some basic signs, and a small American flag lapel pin. The words to *The Star Spangled Banner* were printed on the back.) There were cards for Christmas and Halloween. The Halloween design had a cute jack-o-lantern making the "I love you" handshape. The copy on each was the same. I also had a card to use at New Year's—it had confetti, streamers, and Father Time on the cover.

Because the first impression is so important in making a sale, it's important to have a product with "vibes" that connect with the customer. Choice of trinkets is up to the peddler's preference and experience, but I found that the more creative one's product, the better money it will earn. I peddled at airports for almost eleven years. For most of that time I sold my signature item, the keychain, and only 5 percent of those I approached ever said, "I already have one." I saw the trinkets sold by deaf peddlers all over the country, and I would say there were only fifteen peddlers in the country using the mini-tool keychain.

Don and I had continued to keep in touch as I worked my way across the country, and we still talked to our few friends left at O'Hare. Yet the heyday had ended. They worked secretly, always under the pressure and threat of arrest. In retrospect, it's quite clear that during the late 1980s and early 1990s, our team of peddlers at O'Hare was unknowingly riding the last wave.

# CHAPTER SIX

# Reflections and Renewal

Most peddlers are motivated by a strong aversion to the alternative: working eight hours a day at $5 an hour for years on end. They look at people who work regular hours for low wages and view their situation as a bad deal, a life sentence.

Especially for those with little or no education, receiving the federal minimum seems an absurd alternative to peddling. As they put it, "It stinks!" And in many cases, their view of education is just as negative. They see it as a useless waste of time. "Why get an education," they ask, "when we're earning good money peddling and can make our own hours? When we can decide when we want to work and how long we want to work?"

Peddling can be far more appealing than a "regular" job, despite the fact that peddling can not offer something that a long-term, nine-to-five job does: a way to save money for retirement. Most peddlers who have worked twenty, thirty, and even forty years have no real financial security to look forward to. Without an em-

ployer to put funds into a retirement plan, many peddlers tend to put off saving until it is too late.

Unlike others who are self-employed, deaf peddlers
rarely develop savings plans for emergencies or retirement. Instead, they spend their money on daily (and
often frivolous) needs. Most deaf peddlers do not pay
taxes and are therefore ineligible for Social Security retirement benefits. I know a seventy-six-year-old man
who has been a deaf peddler since he was sixteen . . .
sixty years, imagine that! He never developed a plan to
save for his retirement, and still must peddle to survive.

∞

My peddling money was providing a comfortable income. And it wasn't lost on me that my earnings
weren't going to show up on any W-2 form for the federal government to process. My peddling money was
"under the table," straight cash. On one hand, it was
wonderful; on the other hand, I couldn't quite get rid of
my disdain for the peddling lifestyle.

I thought of successful deaf people who had over-
come communication and attitude barriers to have successful careers. It disgusted me to know that I could do
much better than my current lifestyle. I was just as talented, as educated, and as smart as any other deaf person. I had cheated myself as a person in order to make a
fast buck.

Although I was still peddling full time, at heart I
preferred the way that hearing people seemed to live,
with the knowledge they were going somewhere and
their accomplishments were their own. They could get

up in the morning, go to work, and come home at night with a good feeling about their work. Yes, the money was good, but peddling day in and day out was wearing me down both physically and mentally. It just didn't give me the same feeling of ownership over my life that most hearing people experience.

Though good in many ways, SSDI is a system with tremendous potential for abuse. It has no strict guidelines and no watchdogs. Every time I cashed in my benefit, I felt like somebody had dropped $1,000 in the street and all I had to do was pick it up.

The government has no doubt spent millions of dollars supporting deaf people with attitudes similar to the one I had. After all, why should a person who receives employment-dependent benefits look for a job if he'll only end up making minimum wage? After deductions, one can do just as well, if not better, staying on SSDI. Plus, SSDI includes free medical care.

I have met deaf people across the country who are taking in $2,000 a month from Social Security programs. In 1994, the federal government spent 21.4 billion dollars on SSI for working-aged people with disabilities. In the same year, it spent 33.7 billion dollars on SSDI programs for "disabled workers."[1] It's amazing that the federal government would pay out this much money at a time when the Social Security Administration is wondering about its future.

---

1. U.S. Bureau of the Census. 1996. Statistical Abstract of the United States: 1996 (116th edition). Washington, D.C.: GPO.

Is the government blindly hurting deaf people? Perhaps. And perhaps Social Security programs for deaf people should be eliminated. Certainly these programs are necessary for those who really need them, but does deafness fall into that category? And if it does, then perhaps the government should include an element of community service—picking up trash along the highways, something, *anything* that will help save taxpayers money in other areas. By welcoming so many deaf people into Social Security programs, the government is spending billions of dollars, much of which is wasted.

Deaf peddlers are also hurt by this system. They usually receive SSDI and a tax-free peddling income every month. It seems like easy money. Ted and Lynn, the deaf husband and wife peddling team at O'Hare, have four children. Together, their government benefits came to about $2,000 per month. Add in their extremely generous earnings from peddling, and they enjoyed a nice lifestyle. Did they need that much to live on? Not really. But then, who would turn it down? I saw this repeated over and over, and wondered, *where are the moral values here?*

Yet I was no better. I received SSDI and peddled at the same time. I was as addicted to the system as anyone. So what did that say about my moral values? Part of me knew there were "real" jobs I could do. All I had to do was look at the majority of the hearing people around me. They managed to work, to study, to do whatever was necessary to survive. And my success at college had taught me I had the ability to go as far as I wanted. True, I could be classified as having two disabilities, but even together these disabilities did nothing to diminish my mental capabilities. I knew I could make a good living in the computer field, but the temptation of easy income was too powerful.

Despite the questions I was beginning to ask myself, I continued to peddle—but with a feeling of disquiet and a shadow of guilt. Often, I looked into customers' eyes and saw pity. Pity and sympathy for all the things I couldn't do. And I'd hear that old negative refrain, *can't, can't, can't.* It made me take a big gulp and swallow something that was trying to well up inside me, and it always gave me a slightly sick feeling. Either I was swallowing my pride, or swallowing my disgust . . . not only at myself, but at this person who was daring to feel sorry for me. But then I'd think, *Ah heck, just take advantage of it!* So I kept pushing myself; and the money rolling in helped me to forget the look that diminished me so. In the battle between morality and money, I chose money. And looking at it that way, peddling sounds mighty like prostitution, which I guess, in a way, it is. I didn't sell sex, but I did sell my self-esteem.

Peddling is not only degrading and self-destructive, it changes the way one sees oneself through one's own eyes and through the eyes of others. I constantly wrestled with feelings of inferiority, feeling like a prisoner of the lifestyle. Since leaving O'Hare, I had been peddling on my own. Yet I avoided socializing with everybody, isolating myself even from the deaf community. I wasn't able to go to deaf clubs or deaf gatherings for fear I might run into someone who knew I was a peddler. I was afraid to face the embarrassment of having the issue brought up in front of more respectable deaf folks.

Arriving at the airport in the morning, I often looked forward to the day ahead with distaste. I had to push myself hard to get started and keep going. As the day progressed, I'd get caught up in the activity and push the feeling aside, but on a few occasions, I actually had to drop what I was doing and go home.

My parents had raised me to have a strong work ethic, and hard work had never bothered me. I was not a person without moral values. I did not want to continue to depend on the peddling lifestyle, did not want to contribute to the negative image of deaf people, especially when I knew much greater potential existed for me. It was quite a conflict of values, and I gave it more and more consideration as time went on.

In the airport, I was constantly surrounded by vacationers and business people. I began to think about what it had been like to have a regular job, with employment benefits and money going into a retirement fund, not to mention an even bigger bonus: self-esteem. True, peddling had become difficult and many of my old friends had either given up on it or been sent to jail. But there was much more to my decision than the fear of being arrested. There was the gnawing sense that I had lost my true self, and a growing realization that I had made a bad bargain.

I had placed a price tag on my self-respect, my self-esteem, on my pride, my potential. After peddling on my own for a year, I was beginning to realize that I wanted those things back. I wanted hearing people to look at me with impartiality, not pity. I wanted to end my involvement in supporting a stereotype that I knew quite well was harmful and misleading. I wanted people to see my abilities, my accomplishments, and my strengths—not my limitations.

Although I didn't stop peddling, I began writing in 1995. I thought that putting my experiences on paper would let the hearing public know what they were really buying into when they purchased a peddler's trinket.

When hearing people give money to a deaf peddler, it's important for them to know that they already pay taxes to support the deaf person via SSI and SSDI. In effect, they are making a double donation. There may be the occasional customer who refuses to give because he knows something about deaf peddling and thinks, *That's a lot of b.s., I'm not going to support this guy twice!* But that customer is unusual.

To the customers who give, I say, *Wake up!* Many of these deaf peddlers are earning huge amounts of money from your blind pity and milking the system to live lives of upper-middle class comfort. If you knew that a deaf peddler was earning $500 a day, would you still be eager to donate?

Pity is a positive emotion, but it can have negative effects when it is uninformed. A person who knows what deaf peddling is all about may still choose to give, that's his or her informed decision. But a person who buys a deaf peddler's trinket in a naïve, sympathetic manner is a fool.

∞

As I began writing down my views on peddling, I started to regain some sense of self-esteem and dignity. A year later I began graduate school at the University of Central Florida.

My computer science studies required my full attention, so I had no time for peddling. One of the interpreters for my classes was Rosanne Trapani. We began dating and fell in love. Yet I knew that because she is a CODA (a child of deaf adults), she wouldn't be happy to learn about my dark past as a deaf peddler. So I held off from telling her as long as I could.

Once the first semester ended, however, I decided to take advantage of the lucrative holiday season and return to peddling to pay my bills. Like a smoker trying to kick the habit, I had placed an order for twenty cases about a year ago, telling myself I would quit peddling when the kits were all sold. Before the holidays, I was down to two cases and this peddling run seemed like it was meant to be my last. So I started planning which airport I would peddle at, and began to get ready to go back on the road for one last time.

I told Rosanne where I was going, and why, and she

was shocked. She just couldn't believe that a hard-working graduate student would resort to peddling. I gave her a copy of the manuscript I was working on to help explain, and promised her—and myself—that this would be my last time as a peddler.

Peddling had never been easy. This time, though, it was *much* harder. For several months, I'd assumed the identity of a graduate student, working as a peer with bright colleagues to complete class projects and move toward shared academic goals. Going back to my peddling identity made me even more disgusted with myself than I had been before. I almost went home to spend the holidays with my family, but under the pressure of debt I swallowed my disgust and forced myself through the season.

By January my merchandise had run out, my graduate studies were underway, and my book was getting to its final stage. It was time to get a new life.

Now that I was no longer peddling, I felt as if I had been released from prison. I had been interviewing with different companies all that year, and accepted a job at AT&T Solutions as a Web developer shortly before I graduated—with a 4.0 GPA. Rosanne and I held a church wedding in the spring of 1999 and we're looking forward to having children. I plan eventually to get my Ph.D.

So, you see, a deaf peddler can indeed get another life! I've discovered that there is more to life than material success, and that self-esteem, dignity, and moral values are more valuable than money. I am not, as my fictitious O'Hare traveler in the introduction mused, *a poor deaf guy who can't work.*

The paradox of the deaf peddler arises from misunderstanding, miscommunication, and misinformed attitudes. The long-held belief that the deaf were deficient in many ways sentenced generations of deaf people to unfulfilled lives. But old attitudes die slowly. There are still far too many hearing people who view the deaf as incapable of participating in and contributing to society and far too many deaf people who believe that as well. There are still many hearing people who cannot move beyond pity to equity, and many deaf people who use a history of discrimination and second-class citizenship as a reason to continue cheating both themselves and society.

This cycle can be broken. Ironically, peddling earnings supported the writing of this book. Money given under the false notion that deaf people *can't*, financed a book telling everyone *yes, they can.*